Everybody should Walk a Camino

One Couple's Journey along The Portuguese Way

Diane Neilson

DEDICATION

To my husband, life partner and best friend, Tony.
For doing this with me; for not giving up when it got tough, and for embracing what turned
out to be an extraordinary experience.
May we adventure together for many more years.

To my dad. My first walking partner and the person who introduced me to the great
outdoors. Your presence is sorely missed, and you were fondly thought of every day of our
journey.

And finally, to all of the incredible people we met along the way; you all enhanced our
journey in your own ways and it was a privilege to be a small part of your journey too.

Thank you!

Contents

Introduction

"All truly great thoughts are conceived when walking" - Nietzsche

To walk is to immerse yourself in your environment; in the diversity and beauty of nature in all of its shapes and forms. It is to lose yourself in your thoughts and allow your mind to find its own path and, as a result, shape new and unexpected ideas.

To think, when time is put aside to think, and to expect original thought without the inspiration of the freedom that walking brings, seems to me to be impossible.

Just as walking is a process, so is thinking; and as an extension of that, so is writing.

Not the physical process, which most people do every day without giving it a second thought, but the creative process, and the unexpected evolution of ideas that can be unleashed when given a long path and a clear head. Indeed, the ancient Egyptians did not believe that a thought was a truth until it had been carved into rock and written down.

Walking. Thinking. Writing. A process which has become part of my life. A process which has transcended place, following me from my old urban home, to my new rural home, and to every place that I have ever visited.

Recently, with my husband, I completed the Portuguese Way - a Camino following an ancient route - from the beautiful Portuguese coastal town of Porto, north to Santiago de Compostela in Spain, whose ancient cathedral is the final destination for the many routes taken by pilgrims from all over Europe, and indeed, The World.

The first part of the 'Way' would take us one hundred and eighty kilometres on foot, through the beautiful Portuguese countryside: over ancient roman roads and bridges, past the mediaeval architecture of its villages and towns, churches and monasteries, ancient stone crosses and shrines, following the yellow arrows and scallop shells which have, for centuries, directed pilgrims towards Santiago de Compostela, to the tomb of St James.

On crossing the River Minho into Spain, we would complete the last hundred kilometres through the woodlands and vineyards of the Galician countryside, through the historic cities of Tui, Arcade, Pontevedra, Caldas de Reis and Padrón, before making our final ascent into Santiago de Compostela in time for the midday pealing of the Cathedral bells.

We planned to embrace the pilgrim life: carrying our belongings on our back, staying in pilgrim hostels, known as albergues, eating simple local food, enjoyed as 'pilgrim plates', along the way and immersing ourselves in the camaraderie which inevitably occurs when you have a shared aim, in our case with our fellow walkers. I was also looking forward to some time for reflection; for freedom of thought and the contemplation of ideas brought forth, as one foot follows the other along the pilgrim path.

I had no idea if we could do this. I had no idea if we would enjoy it either, or if it would lead to any unique reflection, and I was certainly not expecting life-changing revelations or enlightenment. I *was* expecting it to be hard - and it was, but it was also rewarding and an experience that I would have no reservations about recommending to anyone.

Chapter 1

Preparation

How do you prepare to walk 248 kilometres? This is a very good question and I did my research.

The practical preparation was in ensuring that we had everything we needed and that it all fit in our backpacks. The other consideration was weight - we had to strike a balance between what we thought we needed and what we could carry, so there were decisions to make: am I really going to have time to read a book or will the kindle on my phone suffice? Do I need to carry a water pack or will a bottle be enough? How many clothes should I take in order to be prepared for both hot and wet weather?

Technical preparation meant downloading an app - we chose 'Buen Camino' which was great, but there are a few to choose from. This allowed us to study the route in advance: find out which of the places we were passing through had a shop, where we could stop for refreshments en-route, and identify potential hostels for each coming night.
It also provided a lot of information about the route itself, including maps, alternative paths, historical information and recommended sights to see. You could plan your route online, altering it as you went along if necessary, and we could always see how far we had gone and how far we had left to go each day. In retrospect, I should have spent a lot more time getting familiar with the app before we left.

Last, but by no means least, I also searched online to read about other people's experiences of walking The Way, and to pick up any practical tips if possible.
A lot of people complete long distance walks, and many of those people are keen to share the ways in which they prepare and to give their advice. However, you would be surprised by how much that advice differs, so you do have to make a judgement call based on your own capabilities. Some people recommend minimal preparation, others suggest walking longer and longer daily distances carrying an increasingly heavy pack for a few weeks before your walk; one person even shared a detailed plan of graduated preparation starting six weeks before the journey. So, with conflicting advice, it came down to two questions: what do I already do that is going to be beneficial, and what more do I need to do?

The countryside where we live is very hilly, so I am used to walking up and down hills on uneven ground, and to wearing boots - as it is usually muddy in parts. I also always carry a backpack, but it is very small - only containing waterproofs, a bottle of water, a snack and my phone.

I know that I am physically fit and healthy and I am used to walking most days, although not twenty kilometres. Usually I walk around eight kilometres, with the occasional longer walk once or twice a week. However, I do have a history of knee problems and had a part knee-replacement operation on my left knee five years ago; it has long since regained its strength and flexibility, but it will be interesting to see how it stands up to daily long-distance walking. I didn't really want to do too much endurance work before I went, in fear of getting an injury - but felt that I should do some in preparation - it was a conundrum.

In the end, I continued my usual daily walks and tried to walk a little further than usual, stuffing my backpack with my sleeping bag and a couple of towels and wearing it whilst I was walking. The weekend before we left for Portugal, I gave my legs a complete rest and made sure that I ate and slept well, and that was about it.

The one thing that people don't seem to talk about online is the physical impact of the walk itself. 'Nobody' mentioned blisters - can you believe that? Nobody talked about the impact of walking day after day with a pack on your back. Nobody mentioned that the first one hundred and forty kilometres are walked completely on cobbled roads. Nobody talked about walking day after day in the hot sun – or the rain; nobody talked about getting clothes clean or dry. And nobody mentioned the noises and smells in dormitories. Maybe these things are thought to be obvious, or maybe they are forgotten - buried beneath the eventual elation of completing the walk. Maybe it's like childbirth - pretty awful but worth it, and then worth repeating.

As we set off from Porto on our first full day on the Portuguese Way, I was optimistic - but also nervous. This was it; we had been planning this and dreaming about it for so long - I really hoped we were ready. I really hoped that the reality would live up to the dream.

Chapter 2

Why now? Our story.

Why now? It's a very good question.

We have always enjoyed a challenge. We go camping as often as the British weather will allow, pitching our tent before setting off on long walks across fells and mountains, and in the past, we have enjoyed sportive events, riding our bikes coast-to-coast across the UK or cycling a hundred miles in a day just for the satisfaction of knowing we can.

Week to week, throughout the year, we walk in all weathers; either driving to a pre-planned location or walking from the back door. Since we have moved to the Ribble Valley we have walked more and more, and with the luxury of endless trails, stunning countryside and dozens of country pubs to walk to, we consider ourselves very lucky.

We have had spells when we have not been able to walk, as we have both had to overcome health issues, but we have always managed to overcome them and continue walking again, picking up where we left off and building up to bigger and better things.

As I mentioned, I had a part knee-replacement operation in 2019, and for years before that had suffered with knee pain, particularly walking downhill. After my operation, I would walk around the local park, at first with crutches and then without, as I built up my strength and stamina again. Six months later, we all went into lockdown as Covid-19 held the world in its grip and the 'daily walk' became almost an obsession. For me, it was a great excuse to go out alone every day and just walk, and it was really the beginning of me writing seriously as well, as I found that ideas for poems and stories would drift into my mind, the inspiration coming from whatever was around me.

Since then, I have never looked back, walking every day and documenting my walks through descriptive recounts, poetry and short stories. On a touring holiday through France in 2023, I recorded our adventures in a daily blog, embellishing the daily descriptions of our walks with poems and stories on driving days, and I think this is what re-ignited my desire to walk a Camino. I say re-ignited because I had long-harboured the idea of doing a long walk, having read every book and watched every film on the subject. I think I had a romantic notion of simplicity; carrying only what I needed, eating when hungry and stopping only when tired, whilst enjoying the meditative ritual of just putting one foot in front of the other with a mind devoid of everyday complications.

Tony has had his own significant challenges to overcome as well. In 2008, after a routine medical at work, he was diagnosed with cardiomyopathy. Although it was a huge shock, and the future felt uncertain, he remained well and was able to maintain his fitness, probably because he was so fit in his younger years. Though his diagnosis was always in the back of our minds, we continued to do the things we have always done: camping, hiking, cycling and walking regularly, and have enjoyed adventuring together on many holidays.

However, in 2022 he suffered a stroke, and although he appeared to recover quickly with no lasting effects, it did make us question how long we would be able to continue doing the things we had always loved to do, walking included. We started to think about the places we wanted to visit and things we wanted to do whilst we were both still well enough and fit enough to do them, and a Camino was high on the list.

So it was that we started to plan more seriously, looking at different routes and reading reviews before deciding on The Portuguese Way. It felt like a huge, but timely, challenge and we were far from sure that we would be able to do it, but we wanted to try.

The rest, as they say, is history, and we were elated to reach Santiago de Compostela after twelve days on the trail. We learned so much about ourselves and met so many amazing people, that despite the hard parts – and there were many – we definitely plan to do another route soon.

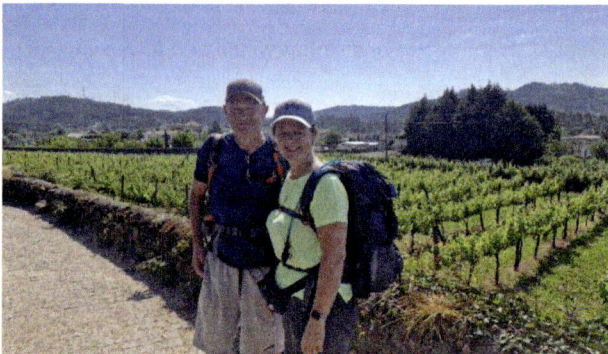

Chapter 3

To be a Pilgrim

We arrived in Porto in the afternoon, and straight away made our way to our accommodation to drop off our rucksacks. We were staying at the Sandeman's Hostel, adjoined to the famous port house, where we have stayed before. But this time, in the spirit of the pilgrimage, we have chosen our first dormitory experience.

Too early to check in, we left our bags in the lock-up and set off to re-familiarise ourselves with this wonderful city.

Rising from the banks of the Douro on both sides, Porto has something for everyone. On the north shore is the historic centre, a UNESCO world heritage site since 1996, with its famous Sao Bento tiled station and the spectacular Clérigos Tower which has far-reaching views of the city, and beyond to the sea; the towering spires of its Cathedral are visible from all around, and there are beautiful old squares and winding streets, whose buildings are adorned with colourful tiled facades and flower-filled balconies.

Crossing to the Gaia district on the south shore requires traversing the impressive Dom Luis metal-arched bridge, where you are treated to breathtaking views of the river Douro from east to west, and of the steep terraced elevation of the city rising from its banks. To the east, there are terraced vineyards as far as the eye can see following the course of the water, and ahead is the Gaia promenade with its imposing port wine lodges, chic restaurants, and cable-car, eventually giving way to the boardwalk trail leading west, all the way to the Atlantic.

Wherever you choose to wander you will be spoilt for choice by Porto's many quaint little shops, street cafes and gardens - and it is even more spectacular at night when it is all lit up, and the traditional Rabelo boats twinkle beneath their fairy lights as they bob on the Douro.

We have been to Porto several times, and with a long walk ahead of us in the morning, chose to stay in Gaia, enjoying a glass of the local Vinho Verde with some food and the glorious views of the river and ancient cityscape in front of us.

As dusk fell, we made our way back to Sandeman's to check in and were shown to our dorm'.

As I said earlier, although we have stayed in hostels many times, we have always booked private rooms and the last time either of us stayed in a dormitory was as a child on school holidays; I don't know what I was expecting - rows of beds or maybe bunks - but it certainly wasn't what I was faced with.

To give some context, the hostel is situated in the Sandeman building, on the upper floors right above the wine cellars, and the historic building and facilities are fantastic.

A large communal area offers a bar, kitchen, large dining table and lots of comfortable seating. With a welcome drink on arrival and complimentary tea and coffee throughout your stay, snacks provided in the afternoon and varied budget-friendly breakfast and dinner menus, you will not go hungry, and the gorgeous old building has been sensitively restored and furnished to pay homage to its age and original purpose. We have stayed here before, in a private room, and it was beautifully decorated with some nice touches such as an old record player with a selection of well-known albums, and with both historic and contemporary pictures on the walls. As in the communal area there were delightful river views out of the window, and we had our own modern shower room.

So, imagine our surprise when we entered the dormitory to see a spacious, bright room fitted with large yellow lockers and modern black steel bunks - it reminded me of the dormitory in the film, Squid Game, although thankfully the bunks were only two high. There were already some occupants, sleeping or reading, although most bunks were still empty, and I was suddenly filled with a sense of giddy trepidation; I didn't know any of these people and I was going to be locked in a room with them all night. How would I be able to sleep? I felt exposed and vulnerable and this was only day one - we had another two weeks of 'another night, another bed' and I wasn't sure I was up for it. It was the first of many 'firsts' but, of course it was fine and we took them all in our stride.

The next morning, we prepared to start our first ever pilgrimage: a two hundred- and forty-eight-kilometre trek along 'The Portuguese Way', from Porto, through the beautiful Portuguese countryside and over the border to Spain. We will head towards Santiago de Compostela, the renowned destination for Pilgrims who travel from all over Europe for the experience; a fortnight of putting one foot in front of the other, day after day; a fortnight immersed in nature, with time to let our minds wander; a fortnight to make human contact with like-minded people; and maybe a fortnight to learn something about ourselves.

I'm not expecting an epiphany, or anything nearly so profound, but I *'am'* looking forward to finding that elusive '*thin place*' and I hope to find a place of peace, contentment and self-awareness within myself.

Here's to our biggest walk yet.

Chapter 4

The Route

Camino means *'path'* or *'way'* in Spanish, and in English, the word camino is often used to mean a pilgrimage or a spiritual journey. The most well-known camino in the world is probably the Pilgrimage Way to the shrine of St James at Compostela de Santiago, in North-West Spain, where tradition holds that the remains of the apostle are buried. To walk there is to make a deeply personal journey, one that has captured the hearts and minds of pilgrims for centuries.

Established after the discovery of the relics of Saint James the Great at the beginning of the 9th century, the Way of St. James became a major pilgrimage route from the 10th century onwards, and in 1492 was officially declared to be one of the three great pilgrimages of 'Christendom', along with *Jerusalem* and the *Via Francigena* to Rome.

In 1987, the Camino, which can be made via several routes through Spain, France, and Portugal, was declared the first Cultural Route of the Council of Europe, and many of the ways have been inscribed on the UNESCO World Heritage List because of their historical significance for Christianity.

Walking the Camino de Santiago is said to be a personal, cultural and physical adventure, whichever route you choose. Most people walk (you could choose to cycle or ride on horseback), but however you choose to travel you will cover an average of twenty kilometres per day and cover between one hundred and five kilometres (Camino Espiritual) and eight hundred kilometres (Camino Frances or Camino del Norte). There are shorter walks, but in order to receive your 'Compostela' from the cathedral, you must complete a minimum of one hundred kilometres and produce your stamped pilgrim passport as evidence.

We chose to walk the central route of the Portuguese Way, from Porto to Santiago, allowing us to visit villages and small towns as we passed through first Portugal and then Spain. At two hundred and forty-eight kilometres, it seemed a reasonable distance for beginners, and if we could keep up the recommended twenty kilometres per day, we would be able to complete it inside of the two weeks we had allowed.

The first part of the route was through the beautiful interior of Portugal, and took us from the cathedral, through the historic city of Porto, until eventually the urban sprawl diminished. Day after day the weather was glorious, the blue sky and sunshine providing the perfect backdrop for a variety of beautiful countryside and the historic treasures dotted along the route.

The first stretch began at the cathedral in Porto and at first, wound its way out of the city on concrete pavements through the historic centre, and then through the suburbs, before finally leaving the shops, cafes and traffic behind to take us along cobbled pathways through farmland. Eventually, after a hot and dusty start, we reached the immense greenery of Vairão, and its beautiful monastery hidden among the ancient trees - our first stop.

The next day was completely different, and we started off by walking through a small woodland, the dirt path following a babbling brook which was to mark the route for several days. The route was flat and the landscape green, but the day felt long and tiring, and we were glad to reach Pedra Furado to take off the backpacks and rest our hot feet.

The next day, refreshed, we walked through Barcelos, a busy town which pays homage to the humble rooster, or 'Galo de Barcelos'. Here there were plenty of cafes offering a hearty breakfast at a pilgrim-sized price which we were happy to take advantage of. With a full tummy, and after stocking up on snacks, we continued towards Ponta de Lima through the glorious vineyards and agricultural land, stopping overnight at Portela de Tamel to break up the thirty-five-kilometre stretch, before arriving at Ponte de Lima with very sore feet at the end of day four. I have since said that I will need to return to Ponta de Lima sometime in the future, as those sore feet and low energy levels prevented me from fully appreciating it.

Although only nineteen kilometres, the next stage, from Ponte de Lima to Rubiães was quite difficult thanks to the steep hike up the Serra da Labruja. The mountain trail, that seems to have been untouched by humans for centuries, is abundant with inspiring natural beauty, and with each step of the steep climb we became almost hypnotised by its peace and tranquillity; it is difficult to imagine that it is the scene of one of the battles of the Napoleonic wars in which the Portuguese ambushed the imperial troops of France. After an equally steep descent down a loose gravel path, we arrived in Rubiães for our last night in Portugal.

The road to Tui was flat and passed through several small villages as we left Valencia behind and approached the international bridge that would take us into South Galicia. Once across the bridge, it was at least another half hour walk along the river and up into the centre, where we would eventually reach the Albergue for our first night in Spain – which is a story in itself as you will see later on, in chapter 13.

From there on it was Spain all the way, and we were eager to get to Santiago. Spain not only brought a change to the language we were hearing and the food we were eating, it also brought about a change in the weather, with a low-pressure system causing a ten-degree drop in temperature and delivering rain almost every day. Despite this, we continued through the Galician countryside, enjoying vineyards, rural villages and beautiful baroque churches, and stopping to rest overnight in Veigadaña, Arcade and Pontevedra, Caldas de Reis and Padrón before finally arriving to hear the midday bells tolling in the cathedral square of Santiago de Compostela, a memory that still gives me goosebumps whenever I think about it.

Chapter 5

Day 1 – Yellow Arrows

Porto to Vairão

Distance walked: 24 kilometres

So, first things first, we survived the 'Squid Game' dormitory. In fact, it was very civilised: a large comfortable bed, locker and charging point; it was also quiet (enough) and we got a good night's sleep - I really need to stop allowing my imagination to run amok!

****

Today was our first day walking and it was mostly a trek through the city, following the map and road signs, as well as the yellow arrows which seem to have been painted randomly onto any available space: walls, lamp posts, telegraph poles, kerbs... you get the idea.

We made our way to the Cathedral in Porto to collect our pilgrim passports, known as the *"Peregrino Credencial"*, which is needed if you want to access hospitality at the pilgrim hostels, or "albergues". It also has to be stamped along the way, daily, as evidence that you have completed the required one hundred kilometres in order to collect the Compostela from the cathedral in Santiago.

The information online recommends one of two routes, the first leading through the city and the second heading towards the coast. We were taking the Central Route, so after taking the obligatory photographs next to the first way-marker, we set off in the direction of the first arrow.

It was not a good start; we followed the first few arrows downhill and walked past Sao Bento Station, before climbing again and hitting a junction. There was no yellow arrow. After consulting the city map, and the app on our phone, we turned left, walking through a large open square and exiting it on the other side to follow the road. Heading north, and using the maps to guide us, we eventually came across a yellow arrow. We were back on track, but

21

already hot, sweaty and slightly frustrated, hoping that our navigation skills would improve.

As I said, not a good start, but a pattern we were to see repeated as the yellow markers were often few and far between when walking through towns. Once out of town they were much better, and it soon became second nature to scan walls, lamp posts and pavements for them as we walked.

There's not a lot to say about a walk through a city - just lots of shops, people and noise - so inevitably, the cogs started turning. The result - a little rhyme that kept my mind busy whilst my feet were feeling the miles add up.

Follow the arrows, uphill and down
The bright yellow arrows that lead out of town
They're painted on street signs, on walls and on posts
And wherever they're pointing - that's where you go

Walking on pavements and old cobbled streets
Through the old city town where Oporto's heart beats
Quaint quintas replaced by a great city sprawl
Where instead of bright tiles, there's graffiti on walls

Follow the arrows along roads and tracks
With feet that are aching and heavy backpacks.
The sprawl becomes suburbs, then villages and trees
The sun beating down and a gentle breeze

So follow the arrows, let your feet lead the way
Hour after hour, and day after day
Forget all the troubles that live in your head
Just enjoy the walk, the good food and your bed.

... which brings me to our accommodation for the night. Once we left the urban sprawl, the main road out of Porto was replaced by cobblestone backroads, leaving behind the dusty outskirts of the city and giving us our first glimpses of the countryside. By this time, we had been on our feet carrying a backpack for about six hours, and were ready for a rest, so we were grateful to arrive at our first pilgrim hostel, the Albergue de Peregrinos do Mosteiro de Vairão.

The hostel opened its doors to pilgrims in 2013, but the building itself dates back over a thousand years and has an interesting history. After its extinction as a religious community in 1891, it was used as a school and college until 1986 and currently has a dual purpose, being used as a holiday centre for the 'cultural promotion of children' and also as a hostel exclusively for pilgrims. It is run by a couple, who once walked the route themselves and, as well as providing refuge for pilgrims, it also raises essential funds to maintain the monastery itself.

As you approach, down a cobbled road, the building emerges ahead of you and is impressive, with it's white-washed three storey facade and towers, church 'Igreja' and necropolis with rows of ornate mausoleums, and a beautiful walled garden. Inside, the decor and design are simple and reflect the monastery's history, and you are immediately enveloped by the peaceful and spiritual atmosphere that permeates the whole space.

We opted to stay in a typical pilgrim's dormitory (wanting to at least start out as authentic pilgrims} and paid our donation. It was not the most comfortable night; the beds were very small and the mattresses hard, reminding me of old black and white films about boarding schools; the sheets we were given were either stored in a freezer or still damp from the laundry, and as it was a cold night we struggled to get warm. There were, however, plenty of old woollen blankets to use, so we piled them on and curled up like mice in a nest. It was very different from our Porto experience, but still very welcome after our long walk.

Boa noite e buen camino.

Day 1: yellow arrows

Following the yellow arrows

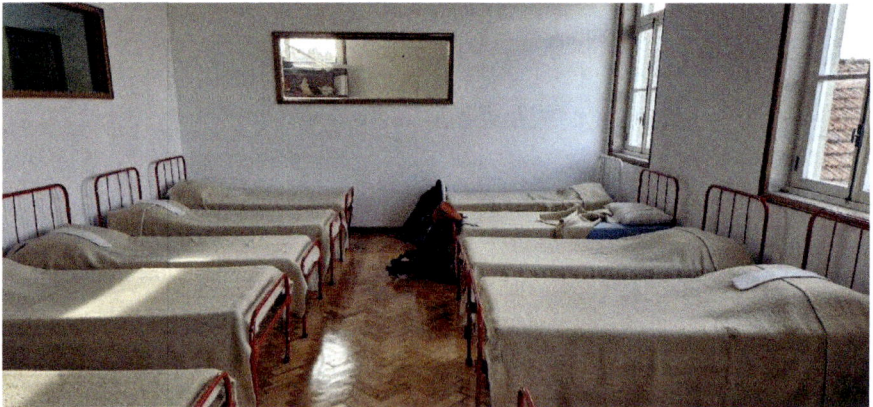

One of the dormitories at the monastery at Vairão

Chapter 6

Day 2 – Cobblestones and Chapels

Vairão to Pedra Furada

Distance walked: 20 kilometres

Rising early, we admired the view from the window of the monastery; the dawn mist lingered beneath a cloudless blue sky and birds were darting between the trees and the eaves opposite. We enjoyed a simple breakfast, chatting easily to other pilgrims, and it was here that we met a Canadian lady who was walking *back* from Santiago after completing the two hundred and forty-eight kilometres with her parents who were both in their seventies. Impressive! - both her and her parents. It certainly stopped us from complaining about our sore feet and helped us to focus our minds on today's route.

If yesterday was defined by 'yellow arrows', then today has been defined by cobble stones: cobbled roads, cobbled paths, cobbled pavements, interrupted only by the occasional stretch of dusty footpath littered with rocks and stones - behaving just like cobbles.

Now cobbles may look pretty, but there is a reason why Edgar Hooley invented tarmac in the early 20th century - they have a terrible impact on vehicular suspension systems, and they are 'very' unkind to feet, so imagine how it must have felt driving a horse and carriage over them.

We retraced our steps up the hill, past the pretty church and its mausoleums, heading out into the lovely Portuguese countryside, a delightful walk passing through beautiful woodland which left us heady with the scent of pine and eucalyptus. We were serenaded by birdsong the whole way, and even managed to catch sight of a Corn Bunting and a pair of Eurasian Spotted Fly-catchers, as well as butterflies, dragonflies and some very noisy frogs.

The route took us through Macieira, through the vineyards that produce the Vino Verde and Brandy of the locality. The layout of the vines was quite unique, the land seemingly split into a patchwork of square small-holdings with the vines planted around the perimeter of the

25

field with a variety of fruit and vegetables growing in the centre, and often a single person was seen tending the land with just a hand-held hoe. This, along with the tethered goats and occasional cow, led me to think that maybe each family provided for themselves with the bulk of the grapes being contributed to a co-operation for production of the local wine, much as we have seen in Madeira. Now this is known to be quite a poor area of Portugal, being outside of the bigger towns and cities, but in my opinion it's not such a poor quality of life: living and working with your family, working your own land and retiring each night to your own home under this beautiful blue sky.

One of the features of today's walk was the lovely São Miguel de Arcos Bridge straddling the River Este, which rushes beneath to swirl around the remains of long disused flour mills and then over the weir to join the Ave River at Espinheiro. A 12th century road. 'Via Veteris', is carried over the bridge, which still shows off its huge ancient stone-slab carriageway and roman arches, unusually, varying in shape - most are typically rounded but a couple are pointed.

Another feature, and one which was to become a recurring theme over the next two weeks, were the many chapels we saw on route.

In Vilarinha, we passed the Chapel de Nossa Senhora da Lapa, and in the adjoining plaza, a three-metre-tall statue of St James as a pilgrim; then in Bagunte, the Chapel of Nossa Senhora de Ajuda, built in 1601.

Further along the road, in Junqueira was the Chapel de Nossa Senhora de São Mamede, dated 1758, and then, close to the bridge, we came across the Church of São Miguel, whose tympanum is pierced by the eyes of an ox.

São Pedros de Rates has a historical district which we almost missed, as it branches left from the trail down an unassuming lane. Our eyes had been drawn to a roadside bar just ahead, however, thirst quenched and hunger appeased, we retraced our steps and walked into the small town to see the Romanesque church of São Pedros de Rates, a listed monument dating from the 12th century and one of the jewels of the day. Close by, we also visited the Chapel de Senhor da Praça displaying several 18th century baroque altarpieces, and the 17th century Chapel de Santo Antonio. Sadly, the door of the latter was closed, but there was a welcoming portico and staircase which provided a few moments of welcome shade from the hot afternoon sun.

More cobbles conquered, and we arrived at Pedra Furada and the parish church of Santa Leocádia with its open belfry. In the portico is a huge stone with a hole pierced in it, and legend has it that this was the tombstone of Leocádia, a saint who was buried alive yet still managed to raise her head and pierce the stone.

The Chapel of Senhor dos Dezamparados *'Lord of the helpless'* is a small, beautifully tiled oratory standing at the side of the road built in 1880, whose roof is topped with ornate crosses and pinnacles. Its purpose is to provide hope and shelter for helpless souls, and there are many more *Alminhas* (outdoor chapels) which are dedicated to the souls of purgatory - along the trail. I am hoping that *'helpless'* and *'purgatory'* are not words that are going to define our experience.

We continued along the ever-undulating cobbled lanes, passing through farming communities and small hamlets. By this time, we were both impeded by blisters, and feeling bullied by cobblestones, so we surrendered and stopped at the O Palhuço Pilgrims Hostel just outside Pedra Furada; we had not reached Barcelos, but had got further than we had anticipated this morning.

However, the day had one more surprise in store for us. As we sat in the sunshine, resting our feet and sharing our thoughts on the day, Tony was subjected to an impromptu 'cooling down' by the sprinkler system, drenching him from head to toe. That will teach him to complain about the heat.

Day 3: cobblestones and chapels

The beautiful São Miguel de Arcos Bridge

Chapel de Senhor da Praça at São Pedros de Rates

The picturesque Romanesque church of São Pedros de Rates

Chapels and Cobblestones

Chapter 7

Feet

Obviously, the care of your feet is an important planning consideration when you are taking on a challenge that requires you to be on your feet for the best part of a fortnight, and for weeks before, I deliberated long and hard about which socks and shoes to wear on this trip.

Boots or trainers is one question, but socks? Who would have thought there were so many options and opinions about socks. Some people swear by merino wool, insisting that they prevent blisters forming, whereas others proclaim that lightweight cotton or bamboo are the best, for the same reason. Anti-blister, moisture-wicking, anti-odour, breathable, thick, thin, cushioned – the list goes on. Then there are discussions about whether you should wear one pair or two; whether you should treat your feet with softeners in the evenings or simply leave them open to the air; whether you should use plasters preventatively, rub petroleum jelly into your feet, wear silicon protectors, the discussions really are endless and everyone seems to have an opinion on the matter.

Then there is the question of which footwear. We do lots of walking; I have been wearing my boots all winter and spring and they fit like a glove. However, I was aware that it would be warmer and drier in Portugal, and that my walking shoes would probably keep my feet a bit cooler. Nevertheless, after a couple of trial walks in my Merrells, I finally decided to stick with my walking boots; after all, they had seen me through the last six months blister-free.

Tony decided the other way and chose to wear his Merrells, his reasoning being that they were more comfortable and cushioned than his boots, and he thought that walking boots would make his feet too hot. Like I said, it's a personal choice.

After two days of cobbles, I was questioning my decision. My feet felt comfortable enough, but I was beginning to collect blisters like badges of honour; under both of my smallest toes (despite using my silicon toe-tectors) and on top of both big toes. After the third day, I also had blisters where the plasters had rubbed which felt really unfair, so the next few days were spent binding, checking and cursing blisters which certainly took the shine off the walking. My free thinking didn't happen, as all I could think about was my sore feet, and as the temperature rose to 29 degrees, *'helpless'* and *'purgatory'* were definitely words crossing my mind and I was beginning to feel mocked by the *Alminhas* along the way.

By day three, Tony also had blisters. Unlike me, he has never suffered from blisters when walking, whatever he is wearing on his feet and however far he has walked. It was a horrible new experience for him as he joined me in the daily quest to find the local pharmacy and the right products.

And we weren't alone. Each evening people were sharing horror stories about their feet and the remedies that work for them: rubbing your feet with Vaseline the night before walking and again in the morning; lotions; creams; strapping all of your toes with plasters; special socks; two pairs of socks; one pair of super-duper very expensive socks; boots; trainers; trail shoes... it was endless. It was also evident that it was very personal and that there wasn't a magical cure. So, we both developed our own very different management plans, and walked on.

The last few kilometres into Ponte de Lima, on day four, were definitely my lowest point and I seriously questioned whether or not I wanted to walk the next day. However, after a good night's sleep and a good breakfast, we decided to carry on... and it did get better, gradually.

On reflection, I don't think it would have mattered which socks and shoes I had chosen. My feet, like everyone else's, simply needed to get used to walking twenty kilometres a day whilst carrying a twenty-pound backpack. And they did. I can honestly say that walking into Santiago after thirteen days consecutive walking, my feet were fine - not a blister to be found anywhere.

Chapter 8

Day 3 – People

Pedra Furada to Portela de Tamel

Distance walked: 14 kilometres

Our journey continued. With sore feet (me) and aching back (Tony), we set off from our Albergue on what could have been quite a 'down' day.

It was very hot, and there was no breakfast on offer today, so by the time we had reached the next village we were ready for something to eat.

Unfortunately, in the tiny hamlet of Carvalhal there was only a bar, and the map informed us that it was several more kilometres to the next village. Fortunately, the kind young man working there recognised us as pilgrims and offered to make us a sandwich, delivering it moments later with fruit juice and coffee; we were very grateful.

We continued, through beautiful countryside and along quiet lanes until we reached Barcelos, quite a large town with a pretty centre – full of roosters...statues of roosters, earthenware and souvenir shops full of clay roosters, tea towels with pictures of roosters on them... roosters everywhere. But why?

Well, of course, there is a story. According to Galician legend, it all started in the 15th century when a Galician pilgrim passing through Barcelos was accused of a crime he didn't commit. Despite his protests, he was sentenced to hang, and in a last-ditch effort, he asked to see the judge, who happened to be having a meal at that time. The pilgrim pointed to a dead rooster on the judge's table and declared that the rooster would crow as a sign of his innocence. As the pilgrim was led to the gallows, something miraculous happened; the roasted rooster stood up on the table and crowed, proving the man's innocence. Astonished, the judge rushed to the gallows and found the pilgrim miraculously alive. He was set free, and the rooster became a symbol of faith, justice, and good fortune.

The people of Barcelos are particularly proud of their cherished emblem that symbolises hope and optimism, but it also holds a special place in the hearts of all Portuguese people and can be found all across Portugal.

Enjoying the atmosphere in the town and the friendly hustle and bustle, we stopped for refreshments and to rest our feet for a while, enjoying the pretty streets and market stalls before continuing through Vila Boa and towards Ribeira, proud of ourselves for having withstood the temptation to buy rooster memorabilia.

At Ribeira, after a long, hot, dusty section of trail, we stopped again for refreshments, and it was whilst we were enjoying another sandwich that a fellow pilgrim approached, throwing himself into a chair and obviously hot and bothered. He introduced himself as Rolf, a German, who had walked thirty-eight kilometres since daybreak, and was struggling with the heat. We were another seven kilometres from the nearest albergue with most of that uphill, so, when it was suggested, he was happy for Tony to book him a taxi. Who would have imagined that Uber would be on hand in rural Northern Portugal. Later, at the albergue, we were reunited and Rolf repaid the favour with a couple of beers over a chat and dinner. Being a six-times annual pilgrim of this route, he also told us that the first three days on the Camino were the hardest - here's hoping!

A little earlier, on that final uphill stretch, just as I was really beginning to regret not getting in the taxi with Rolf, we caught up with a pair of walkers who had stayed at the same hostel as us last night. They were a mother and son duo from Brazil called Eliana and Felipe, and we started up a tentative English-Portuguese exchange. That conversation (Felipe's English being about as competent as my Portuguese) probably saved me, as my brain was so busy thinking about communication that it didn't have time to worry about my throbbing feet; another kindness, intended or not.

One of the things I was looking forward to on this journey was connecting with like-minded people, and so far, we had tentatively reached out to quite a few along the way. People who had started out from the cathedral at Porto on the same day seemed to walk similar distances and therefore stop at the same hostels; people from Canada, Australia, Brazil and from all over Europe. We engaged in many polite conversations whilst walking as our paths crossed and were witness to many more, as people were keen to tell their stories and hear about others' reasons for walking. We chatted over pilgrim plates in roadside cafes between places, we shared our experiences and advice over injuries at the albergues in the evenings, and we then all settled down to sleep, head-to-head and toe-to-toe, in bunk-beds and dormitories. Strangers - but not; united in our shared challenge.

This made me think about all the times we had been camping as a family; people used to ask me how I could sleep at night with just a sheet of canvas between us and the rest of the world; how we could leave camp for the day with just a zip between all our worldly belongings and whoever might want to enter and take them; how we could let our small children play in woodland with other children whose families we had never met and didn't know. And whilst some people may have thought me naïve, I have always felt safe camping; safe among friends – fellow campers; like there was a code of honour that we were all in it together and would look out for each other; that another camper would never dream of doing anything that would harm one of their own.

And this is how it felt 'en-camino'. There was a camaraderie - a pilgrim's code of conduct, and it allowed me to feel safe in those dormitories, with all those strangers. Strangers who would lend you their phone charger, share their food and toiletries with you and spend time listening to your story and getting to know you, even though your lives may never cross again.

Along the way, over the course of those two weeks, I certainly learned to talk less and listen more. I found that listening to other peoples' stories is almost always more interesting than retelling your own over and over again, and that you nearly always learn something, for everyone has a story to tell.

Today, through my difficult Portuguese conversation with Felipe, the determination to find the words that we needed to communicate made our physical journey up that hill just a bit easier, and might have been the difference between making it to the top, or not.

So, if you were part of my journey today, thank you - you made a difference.

Day 3: People

A welcome pit-stop in the beautiful town of Barcelos

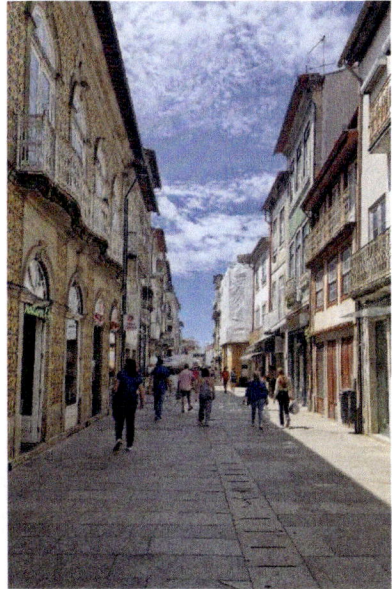

Chapter 9

What's in a backpack?

What do you really need for two weeks of walking?

It should be a simple question, with simple answers, but when I started considering all the possibilities: weather, terrain and access to daily supplies, I realised that it wasn't going to be easy. There were going to have to be compromises.

I started off with an *'ideal world'* list, and then I questioned everything on that list.

Is it essential?

Is it the best option?

Do we need one each?

Is there a lightweight version?

Can I manage without it?

You get the idea!

Then there is the obvious consideration – I have to carry it all. Will it fit in the pack? And suddenly, things you think you can't do without become non-essential. It's an interesting process to go through and really made me question what I could and couldn't do without.

First of all, we had to sleep. And we didn't know where we would be staying beyond the first night in Porto. From my research, I knew that albergues were very variable, ranging from a basic bunk in a shared dormitory, to the luxury of a private room. We had already decided that we wanted to complete our Camino as authentically as possible, staying in the traditional albergues, which meant that it was more than likely that we would have to provide our own bedding. A sleeping bag was the obvious option, but ours were four-season camping bags, weighing far too much and taking up far too much space in our backpacks. We needed to buy lightweight single season bags.

Did we need a pillow? I thought so, until I tried to fit it in my back pack, then I changed my mind – a rolled-up jumper would do. In the end, it turned out that even the most basic of accommodation provided you with a pillow, along with a disposable sheet and pillowcase, which solved that problem.

Nightclothes? I settled for a very lightweight pair of shorts and a vest-top but also packed a pair of leggings just in case it was cold. A light jumper would have to double up as a pyjama top if necessary.

Clothing. This was tricky. We would be walking in mid-May and weather records told me that it should be warm and dry – great! However, another site said that May was unpredictable, and when it was wet could be a lot cooler – not so great. The reality is that in northern Europe, May can be unpredictable, so we had to pack for both warm and cold, and wet and dry weather, and as it turned out we had a hot, dry first week and a much cooler, wetter second week. The other problem would be getting clothes dry overnight when it did rain, so I did some research to find the best walking gear for 'through walks', which is the term used for longer walks over several weeks or months. Whilst there was plenty of advice, once again it was variable, with some people preferring ordinary walking clothes (to suit the season) along with waterproofs to wear over the top, and others preferring clothes made in 'quick-dry' fabrics. That still left the question of rainwear; I didn't really want to carry a coat, but I didn't want to get soaked either, should it rain. And what about the evenings? Did I really want to be clodding around in boots and walking gear after a shower? Lots to ponder.

I finally decided on three sets of lightweight clothes, a hoodie, a kagool and a pair of flip-flops. It seemed minimal. It was minimal - but necessary, and it was enough. Yes, some days - especially in the second week - it rained, or there was no washing machine at the hostel, or the drier wasn't working. We may have smelled slightly unpleasant and I may have had to walk with underwear hanging drying from my pack; but everyone was in the same boat, so nobody really cared.

Then there was everything else. We would be walking for around six hours a day, which left a lot of time to fill. What would we do in our down-time? Wash our smalls, listen to music, read a book? There would certainly be time to kill, and we probably wouldn't feel like pulling our boots on and exploring after twenty kilometres on the road.

I uploaded a couple of books and packed my kindle. Then I unpacked it – I could access kindle on my phone. My phone could also play music to me. I then realised that my phone was going to be very busy: providing maps for me during the day, helping us to find places to eat and shop, writing my daily blog, and now being my entertainment in the evenings. I decided to buy a powerpack and I was glad I did; it was a godsend on a couple of occasions when there was no charging point available at the hostel, or when the battery suddenly dropped in the middle of nowhere.

We would need a couple of washing-powder tablets, toiletries and towel, and a first aid kit. Suncream, a hat and sunglasses for those sunny days. A bum-bag was useful, for keeping our money and passports safe, and earplugs – don't forget the earplugs! Those dorms can be noisy places.

And last but not least, the back-pack itself. Most of the articles that I read said that you should carry no more than 20% of your own weight – and that includes the pack. I chose a lightweight 40L pack with plenty of pockets and a rain-cover, and I also bought a pack of small carabiner clips which were really useful for attaching stuff to the outside – particularly wet washing when the drier at the hostel was out of order. Once packed with everything on my list, my pack was less than the recommended 20% so I was feeling quite smug – until I picked it up! It felt really heavy and I seriously doubted that I would be able to carry it for even one 20-kilometre stretch, never mind fourteen consecutive days, but I didn't feel that I had anything that was surplus to requirements, so I would just have to get used to it.

Kit list
Lightweight backpack with rain-cover and some small carabiner clips.
Lightweight sleeping bag, shorts and vest top, pair of leggings.
3 each of: walking shorts, quick-dry t-shirts, underwear. 1 lightweight jumper, a kagool, a pair of flip-flops.
Mobile phone, charger (with EU adaptor), powerpack.
Travel size 2-in-1 shampoo and conditioner, shower gel, toothpaste, toothbrush, multi-use razor.
A lightweight sports towel, high factor suncream, peaked hat, sunglasses, earplugs.
First-aid kit: lots of plasters, plaster roll, blister plasters, a bandage, Vaseline, painkillers, a needle and thread (for blister treatment*), antiseptic cream.
Bum-bag
Hydration gels for emergencies. On a more isolated trail you would have to carry food, and maybe cooking equipment, as well.

As it turned out, the backpack didn't turn out to be a problem (even when I had to add water, which I had forgotten to include, and is surprisingly heavy). Once it was well adjusted it felt quite comfortable, and I quickly got used to it. What I hadn't considered, is that all that extra weight has to go through your feet, and that was much harder to get used to.

* Needle and thread treatment for a blister

This is a trick I've used for years and really works, but unbelievably, I forgot to take a needle and thread with me on this trip. As a result, I suffered horribly for about five days, until I finally found a chemist that would sell me a needle.

If you get a blister which is typically filled with fluid, the one thing that you want to do is to pop it, the problem being that it just refills again – your body's way of protecting the new skin forming underneath. The other problem is that if you tear the damaged skin, you end up with a really sore wound for days afterwards.

One way of avoiding both of these problems is by using a needle and thread.

1. First, sterilise both the needle and thread by soaking in some boiling water.

   (I used a thread of cotton pulled from a frayed sock)

2. Carefully, thread the needle and pass it through the blister, entering on one side and exiting on the other.

3. Remove the needle, leaving the thread running through the blister. This keeps the two pinprick holes open and allows the fluid to drain, whilst the skin re-adheres itself to the wound, often healing perfectly.

4. Apply a plaster or bandage for 24 hours or until the wound stops weeping then remove the thread and re-cover with a fresh plaster.

Ta dah! No more blister.

I'm not offering any guarantees, but it works for me.

Chapter 10

Day 4 – Toughing it out in Paradise

Portela de Tamel to Ponte de Lima

Distance walked: 22 kilometres

Today was hot; really hot – *'muito quente!'* Not only was it hot, but we were aware that this was a long stretch of the trail, and that the route would take us through largely unshaded countryside, so there would be no escape from the heat of the sun. An added concern was that there were very few refreshment points marked on the map so we had to carry a lot of water.

Add to that our ailing feet and our status as Camino novices, it's fair to say that we felt quite daunted. So, with some trepidation, we plastered and strapped our feet, filled our water bottles, donned suncream and hats, and set off on the next stage of our journey.

An hour later and it was 25°. We stopped for breakfast at a roadside cafe, joining half a dozen other 'Peregrinos' who had taken respite from the heat. The topic of conversation (after introductions) was riveting: footwear, sore feet and blister remedies - we all contributed.

An hour later, fed and watered, the temperature had risen to 28° and we all set off, soon spreading out along the trail, each walking at our own pace.

Despite our sore feet and the unforgiving cobbled paths, our breath was taken away by the stunning scenery along the way; a picturesque backdrop of distant mountains, trees and agricultural land, interspersed with traditional stone cottages and beautiful swathes of wildflowers.

We wandered along at a leisurely pace, enjoying being between the vines, looking at the great diversity of flora and listening to the uplifting sound of birdsong. We even came across a large lizard, sunbathing and showing off its beautiful colours, and a nanny goat with her three newborn kids, all willing to pose for photos.

With five or six miles left, we were flagging. So, hot and tired, we made our way towards the only remaining cafe en-route, and just before, on the left, there was a beautiful old olive tree, adorned with Camino tokens and good wishes for pilgrims; there was also a shady bench with an invitation to rest, complete with a jar of sweets to boost the passing weary travellers - it was really quite wonderful!

Refreshed, we continued, and six 'very tough' miles later, we made our final approach towards Ponte de Lima, renowned for being one of the loveliest and best-preserved towns in the whole of Portugal, named after the spectacular medieval bridge that spans the river. I wish I could say that I noticed.

The final mile along the south bank of the river, seemed to go on forever; my feet were in agony, with blister upon blister. It was 'so' hot and I was parched having drunk the last of my water a mile back; my back was aching and for the first time, I was really questioning the wisdom of this trip – after all this was only day four. I think a snail could have crossed that bridge faster than I did, and I was certainly in no state to appreciate several spectacular riverside statues drawing you towards the beautiful old-town, huddled around the remains of the old keep.

I cannot begin to describe how tired I was; it was certainly a relief to arrive at the albergue on the other side of the river, have our passports signed and collapse gratefully onto a narrow, hard, plastic-covered mattress in a long dormitory, where I remained for the next two hours.

Later, showered and somewhat rested, hunger got the better of us and we did venture out, working our way through the maze of narrow cobbled streets and gazing at the delightful centuries-old mansions built in an amazing variety of styles, from romanesque to gothic, baroque to neoclassical. Weary and somewhat forlorn, we came across a small restaurant, filled with locals. It was the only eatery we had come across this side of the bridge - and it was full. I couldn't face crossing that bridge again and we had resigned ourselves to remaining hungry, but as we turned away, the waiter came outside and beckoned us over. That man saved the day, creating a small space for us and bringing us food and wine of his own recommendation, as we couldn't understand the menu. The food was wonderful and the atmosphere was lively, full of local people – families and friends – having a wonderful time in an amazing place.

As we were warmed, the food and wine feeding our souls as much as our bellies, we reflected on our journey so far; it's tough - tougher than we could have imagined, and yet somehow today, despite all the discomfort, I know that my enduring memories will be of the people we met, conversations had and the sights and sounds we encountered along the way... and that waiter! I hope one day I can go back and thank him, for he can't possibly know how much his kind gesture meant to two hungry, weary pilgrims at the end of a very long, hard day.

Day 4: Toughing it out in Paradise

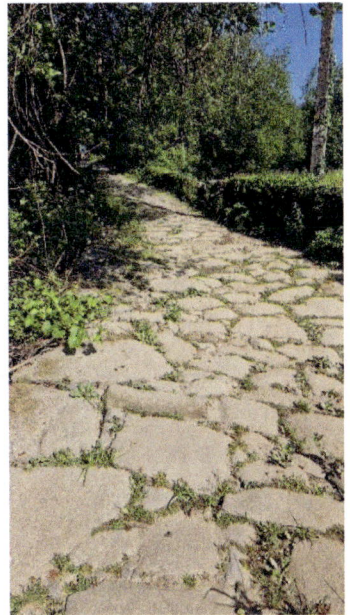

Some of the stunning Northern Portuguese countryside between Portela de Tamel to Ponte de Lima

Chapter 11

Best laid plans...

Being sensible walkers, and also being aware of our age, inexperience and limitations, we started out with a plan: to walk for two or three days then have a rest day. We thought that if we repeated this pattern, we should be able to not only complete the walk, arriving in Santiago de Compostela within the two weeks, but to enjoy it and avoid picking up any niggling injuries.

So, our loose plan was this:

Day 0 – to spend a day in Porto

Days 1-3 – to walk to Ponta de Lima

Day 4 – to spend a day in Ponta de Lima and stay in a B&B; a little treat

Days 5-6 – to walk to Tui

Day 7 – to spend a day in Tui and stay in a B&B; another little treat

Day 8-9 – to walk to Pontevedra

Day 10 – to spend a day in Pontevedra; can you have too many treats?

Day 11-12 – to walk to Padrón

Day 13 – to spend a day in Padrón; I know...

Day 14 – to walk to Santiago de Compostela

Best laid plans, hey...

The trouble is that you get hooked.

For the first few days, we thought that if we didn't keep getting up and walking, we might be tempted to quit, as we were plagued by blisters. So, we just put our heads down and carried on walking.

When we arrived in Ponte de Lima we were in a bad way, both mentally and physically. It had been far harder than we had imagined – the backpack, the blisters, the heat, the cobblestones – and I think we were both almost ready to accept defeat. However, we decided to leave the decision until morning, and when I asked Tony what he wanted to do, over breakfast, he said, "Let's just walk." So we did.

44

And that became our mantra, 'Let's just walk'.

We didn't even talk about rest days after that, and never again thought about giving up, but what we did do was adapt our route. The app we used was great, providing a daily pre-planned suggested route which informed you of all the sights along the way, as well as cafes, bars, hostels and B&B's. However, some of the daily stretches were much longer than others and so we decided to create our own route – one that suited us.

The Buen Camino app that we used does allow you to personalise your route, so we sat down together and studied it, taking note of all the places that had accommodation along the way, giving ourselves early opt-out options should we need them, and we walked shorter and more even, stretches each day.

The sense of achievement was tremendous. Each night, we took stock of how far we had walked, how we felt, what we had seen and who we had talked to, and we planned the next day's walk.

We were back in control, but we weren't injury free; Tony had to buy new trainers in Tui and was continuously adjusting his pack to accommodate his achy back, and I developed an annoying knee injury three days from Santiago, but we kept going. We walked at our own pace and rested as often as we could, probably frequenting most of the rest-stops on the way.

Where we could, we stayed at one of the local albergues, but once or twice we did pay a little bit more and stayed somewhere more comfortable, not just as a treat, but because it fitted in with how far we wanted to walk.

In retrospect, this is what we should have done from the beginning, and what I would advise anybody else to do. Walking a Camino is not a race to the finish, and although the apps provide good guidance, it is just that – guidance, and you should walk at your own pace.

As a result of the changes we made, we completed our Camino in twelve days and walked into Santiago de Compostela at the ringing of the midday bells after a short eleven-kilometre final stretch. And what's more, we walked in with friends; friends we would never have met had we stuck to the original plan.

So 'Buen Camino!' Enjoy the experience at your own pace and in your own way.

Chapter 12

Day 5 – Walk, Eat, Sleep. Repeat.

Ponte de Lima to Rubiães

Distance walked: 21 kilometres

If you had told me 24 hours ago that I would have walked again today, I wouldn't have believed you. Last night I was exhausted; everything ached and my feet felt like they had been run over by a truck.

But after a couple of hours flat on my back, and an honest review of the situation over a lovely meal at the little tapas restaurant we found in Ponte de Lima, we had a decent night's sleep, accepting that today may need to be a rest day.

So, in the morning we packed our things and found somewhere for breakfast. After perusing the map, weather forecast and Buen Camino app, Tony said to me, "Let's just walk."

So we did. We recrossed the medieval bridge and started to follow the yellow arrows.

It's really important when walking with a partner, or in a group, that a certain etiquette is followed: the slowest person should set the pace; a rest should be taken when anybody needs one; and you should have a range of endpoints planned so that you can stop for the night as soon as the first person in the group signals 'enough'. There is no judgement; we all have our own pace, level of fitness and stamina and everyone is respected.

With this in mind, we planned to complete the next leg to Rubiães, with several options for an early finish.

The route was varied, at first winding through villages and then through fields along the ever-present cobbled paths. There had obviously been some rain overnight, as water poured from the fields to puddle the paths along the way, and at one point, we had to leave the path (which had become a river-bed) and make our way cautiously through the boggy field, as a

46

young man from the group ahead stood on the bridge at the end shouting instructions to us. The bog navigated successfully, we crossed the road and left the valley. As we began to climb, we entered the forest: luscious greenery, rushing rivers and some spectacular, tumbling waterfalls, all a result of the recent rainfall, no doubt. You do have to remember that without the copious amounts of rainfall in northern Europe, we wouldn't have our stunning, verdant countryside.

This was 'our' terrain - mountain trails and winding dirt paths - even a boggy stretch to make us feel at home. Before long, as promised, the path began to climb. We had a steep ascent followed by an equally steep descent before us, and it looked tough.

We took a break at a roadside cafe, to refuel, adjust our packs and footwear, and top up our water bottles, and then set off with steely determination.

The climb began steeply and just kept getting steeper, and for four kilometres we scrambled over rocks and boulders, passing memorial peregrino way-markers; familiar stone crosses adorned with messages, mementos and Camino memorabilia. As I climbed, I found myself chanting the familiar verses of 'The Gruffalo' in rhythm to the movement of my feet - over and over again - until finally, we arrived at the top. Thank you, JD!

Then the descent; I really would rather go uphill than down. A similar distance, but thankfully less steep, our feet slipping and sliding on sandy pebble paths, until at last we reached the foot of the hill.

From there it was an easy walk into the village of Rubiães, where we registered at the Albergue and enjoyed a delicious 'pilgrim's plate' at a local restaurant down the road.

I felt a real sense of achievement today, after last night's low point, and thought that maybe we could do this after all!

Day 5: walk, eat, sleep, repeat

A day of muddy paths,   steep mountain trails...

... and lots of camino memorabilia along the way to keep our spirits up

Chapter 13

Pilgrim Plates

We had no idea what we would be eating along the Portuguese Camino, but we had read about Pilgrim Plates, meals served in local eateries at pilgrim prices. These meals are served three times a day, at breakfast, lunch and dinnertime, however, as we found, people are always happy to make you a sandwich and a coffee if you arrive outside of meal times. I also assumed that these plates would be very different depending whether you were in Portugal or Spain, and I have to say, it was one of the things that I was most excited about.

The other tradition I had read about, and was looking forward to, was participating in shared meals with other pilgrims. I had seen films and read wonderful stories about albergues and bunk-houses, where everyone contributed to the evening meal; preparing, cooking and eating together, sharing stories and discussing the day's walk over a glass of the local wine. I'm sad to say that this didn't seem to happen very often, despite all of the hostels we stayed in having great cooking and eating facilities. Maybe people were too tired to contemplate cooking at the end of a long day, or maybe the local restaurant options were just too good to pass up; I can see both being possible, but it's a shame we didn't get to partake in that particular element of Camino life.

So, we knew that we would be able to find food, but what we didn't know was what would be on the menus, or what the quality of the food would be like. The truth is that the menus were very variable and quite limited, but were always tasty, filling and great value for money. I wasn't going to lose any weight on this walk, whatever the mileage.

Each morning, we would start walking before stopping at the first café we came across for breakfast. Typically, we were served orange juice, a ham and cheese sandwich and coffee, for around five euros, which would keep us going until lunch time, although there were variations such as, 'pan con tomate' (toasted baguette with pureed tomato), or 'pan con mermelada' (toast with jam or marmalade).

There were usually snack bars along the way where you could top-up with a slice of tortilla and a drink, but the main meal was served around lunch time and was usually a set menu, consisting of: a starter of soup, salad, or fish, a main course which was some sort of fish or

49

meat with chips or potatoes and bread, and a dessert, usually the local cake or ice cream. There was also a drink included – a flagon of wine, beer or water – and all for between ten and twelve euros per person, which was amazing value.

You would have thought that another meal would be unnecessary wouldn't you, but by the time we had spent another four hours putting one foot in front of the other, we were always starting to think about our stomachs again, and about what 'tapas' or 'pintxos' would be on offer that evening. Like I said, if you walk a camino don't expect to lose weight.

Dinner is often served around 6–7pm in local restaurants, and again, if there is a pilgrim plate it will be another three courses with wine. Whilst the quality of the menu varies, it remains remarkable value, and whilst choice can be limited in small towns and villages, there are more options in cities and towns, with the additional option of paying a bit more for a restaurant meal.

This happened to us in Padrón. We had showered and changed at the hostel and set off to find something to eat. As we were a little early (most restaurants don't start serving until 7pm), we bought a drink and sat outside in the early evening sunshine, a welcome change from the rain that had seemed to follow us for the previous couple of days. After our drink we wandered around looking at window menus; we had already decided to splash out a bit on a nice meal and were eager to peruse the options. In a square, we came across a small restaurant. There was another couple looking at the menu, and a few other people just stood waiting. As the clock struck seven, the doors opened with a flourish and a small, plump man beckoned the first couple in before shutting the door again. We looked at each other, perplexed, but nobody else seemed surprised. Intrigued, we decided to wait it out – he had piqued our interest. One by one, the couples were ushered inside and each time the doors closed, until at last it was our turn. When we entered, the couples who had gone before us were seated, with a drink. Nobody had menus. The waiter seated us and did bring us a menu, followed quickly by a drink. He asked what we would like to eat, and as the menu was all in Spanish, we asked for his recommendations. That was the last we saw of the menus; he very quickly decided what we should have and scurried off to give the order to the chef. We hadn't a clue what we were going to get, but it was all delicious, beautifully presented, and although pricier than what we had been used too, not too expensive and a real treat.

As we ate and drank, the remaining tables in the restaurant filled up, with one – a table set for six – seating a woman dining alone. That was that! One cover and first come-first served. As we were leaving, another couple followed us out and asked if we had enjoyed our meal. We confirmed that we had, and commented on the colourful character and quirkiness of the waiter. He was the only member of staff we saw, but was very helpful and attentive and seemed very invested in his customers, doing everything he could to optimise their experience, but without being overly attentive. We had been lucky. The couple told us that the waiter was the owner and he had previously owned a Michelin-starred restaurant in one of Spain's big cities. He tired of the busy city life and had moved to Padrón to open this small business, which he ran exactly how we saw tonight, every night. It was open from 7pm for one cover only, first come-first served and closed again by 10pm. The food was always amazing and the service was as you would expect from someone so highly acclaimed in the restaurant world... and he never turned anyone away just to turn a bigger profit; hence the single lady at the table for six was treated as graciously and with as warm a welcome, as everyone else. What a brilliant story!

Chapter 14

Day 6 – Let's go to Spain

Rubiães to Tui

Distance walked: 17 kilometres

The albergue at Rubiães was OK but we did have a bit of bad luck with our laundry today. I put some dirty clothes in to wash before we left to eat and, when we returned, we found the display flashing 'out of order'. We were left with a mess of unwashed, sodden clothes which we had to hang up to drip dry.

Of course, they weren't dry in the morning so we had to hang as many as we could off our packs and stick the rest in a carrier bag (the drier wasn't working either).

It hadn't been a great night's sleep either; the dorm was full, with twenty-four people making the noises and smells that sleeping people make - until 5.30am that is, when they all started to get up and go, leaving us with two hours of peaceful slumber.

On a more positive note, we both felt that our feet were less sore, so set off with a bit of a spring in our step. We also came across a cafe-cum-convenience store not far down the road and enjoyed freshly squeezed orange juice, a coffee and a sandwich, giving us just the energy boost we needed.

As we have now come to expect, we soon rejoined the cobbled path that has come to define the Portuguese section of the 'Camino de Santiago Way'.

We relaxed into the walk, which took us through woodland paths running in tandem with freshwater streams, and fields strewn with flowers. We crossed two ancient roman bridges, passing over fast-running rivers with water as clear as glass, and stopped to look at the waterfalls, chapels and stone crosses along the way.

After an initial short climb, the path was mostly downhill, sometimes steep, but more often gently rolling downwards. Eventually we began to pass more and more houses, and then larger buildings as we entered Valença, the most northern part of Portugal on the south side of the River Minho. We followed the yellow arrows through the pretty old town, slowing down to browse in the shops and longing to stop at one of the street cafes.

The route then took us up again, winding through the ruined fortifications (very similar in style to the ones we saw at Neuf-Brisach in France the year before), where there were lots of people picnicking or sunbathing on the grass. We were tempted to join them, but Spain was beckoning, so we made our way down the narrow streets to the Tui International Bridge, a strange, metal, latticed structure flying across the River Minho to join two countries - one foot in Portugal and the other in Spain.

The bridge's clever design allows cars to travel through the central hollow whilst trains travel above, with footpaths for pedestrians along either side. We chose the right-hand walkway (as recommended by Mary, a fellow walker from California), and enjoyed views of the cathedral and Old Town of Tui as we entered Spain.

That should have been that - find the albergue, eat, sleep, repeat - but life's not like that is it.

We went out and had a lovely meal in the main square of the old town - tapas and a nice bottle of wine - arriving back at the albergue about an hour before locked doors (they are very strict about these things).

But we had made a huge mistake. We hadn't realised that the time zone had changed as we crossed from Portugal to Spain, and instead of being fifty-five minutes early, we were actually five minutes late. The door was locked, and despite us banging on the door and shouting up at the dormitory windows, no-one answered; all our stuff was inside, including our phones which we had left charging.

We then spent a frantic half an hour trying to explain what had happened and ask for help, to anyone who would listen, but it was getting late and nobody spoke English. Eventually, I managed to communicate in Portuguese with a Spanish lady called 'America' (that's not a typo) closing up her café. She was an angel; she phoned around the hostels until she found one with beds and then arranged for the owner to meet us there; she even walked with us to show us the way.

Once gratefully settled, we managed to grab a few hours rest before returning to collect our belongings from our original lodgings.

What an evening! Chocolates ordered and on the way to America.

Day 6: let's go to Spain

Saved by America.
I hope she got the chocolates

A walking clothes horse – I wasn't the only one!

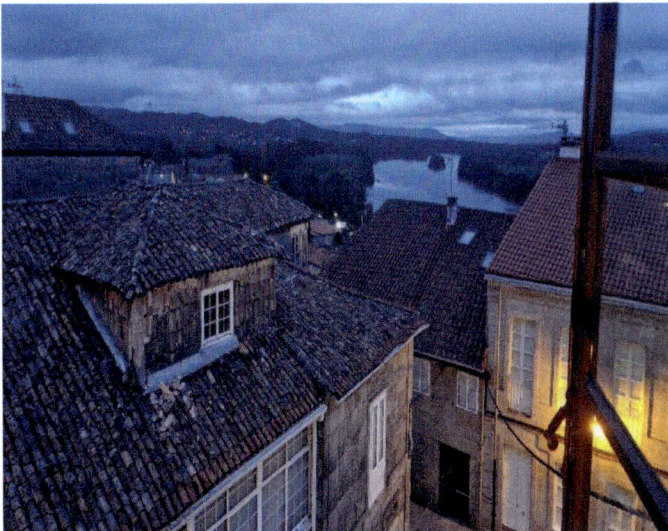

A view of the sunrise from the albergue at Tui.

It's a shame we didn't get chance to stay there.

Chapter 15

The Australians

On the Camino you meet all sorts of people from all over the world, and it is always interesting to hear their stories; finding out what has prompted them to complete a pilgrimage and why they have chosen to travel – sometimes a very long way – to do so. For some people there are religious or spiritual reason and for others, the reason is more personal – linked to illness, bereavement or their personal lives. Others just want to walk, to immerse themselves in nature and enjoy a new experience.

We found it surprising that we encountered so many Australians walking The Portuguese Way, and I was eager to find out their reasons for travelling so far to complete what is really, just a long walk.

One such couple were a father and daughter team. They seemed very comfortable with the walking and were very gregarious; eager to chat with the other 'Aussies' they came across, but also happy to spend time with other people as well. I had listened from my top bunk as they shared stories about their homeland, comparing lifestyles and experiences with other Australians, and also in a cafe where they entered into heated political discussions about world affairs with an Asian couple and a Brazilian man.

It was a couple of days later, however that I fell into conversation with the daughter and asked why she and her dad were doing this together. She laughed, initially avoiding the question and saying that her dad was 'just there to check up on her' and 'cramp her style', but then she began to talk about her real reasons for walking.

She said that she had excelled at school and was also very sporty, and had left home to go and study at university, which she enjoyed at first. But by the time she had gained her degree she had felt more and more lost, not knowing what she wanted to do next and having no clear direction or an interest in any particular career. Talking about it, she said, seemed to make things less clear, and as her parents had separated, she felt that she didn't want to go back to either of their homes when her course finished. She decided instead, to take a gap year and travel to Europe to walk the French Way, hoping that 800 kilometres of contemplation would give her some direction and help her to decide what she wanted to do with her life. That was two years ago. She said that she didn't know whether she was 'hooked on walking' or just avoiding real life, but she had moved on from one camino to another, walking all of the Santiago routes. She had just kept on walking. She said that she enjoyed the nomadic lifestyle and didn't feel ready to put down roots, preferring to move from place to place and meet new people along the way.

Her dad had flown out for a visit, and was walking The Portuguese Way with her. She implied that he was helping her out financially, but was getting impatient and hinting that it was time for her to 'settle down', which she still didn't feel ready for.

I wondered how long she would keep on walking, and where her travels would take her. I never really talked to her dad so didn't have a perspective on his feelings, but I hope they came to a supportive understanding and that she manages to find some peace and direction.

Chapter 16

Day 7 – The Power of Positive Thought

Tui to Veigadaña

Distance walked: 23 kilometres

After yesterday's comedy of errors in Tui, and the weather forecast promising rain all day, it would have been easy to book a B&B and have a day off - I think we both thought about it.

We had to set an alarm for 6am (not very 'us') so that we could return to our original albergue at the monastery to collect our backpacks and phones. I was hoping to speak to somebody about what had happened, as I did think it would make sense for them to point out the time differences to pilgrims as they arrive – surely we weren't the only ones to have made that mistake.

Nobody was on duty at the reception, however, but I did leave a note of my own on the noticeboard – very politely worded, I promise.

One positive that came from all this was that we saw our first sunrise, and with that I decided that this was going to be a good day.

So here are all the things that made us feel thankful today:

❤️ We saw a beautiful sunrise.

❤️ There are some very kind people, to whom we are very grateful. Thankyou America, we hope you enjoy the chocolates, and have left a great review for your café.

❤️ Thank you also to the lady who runs the 'Albergue Buen Camino', in Tui, for returning to work 'out of hours' and sorting us out with a bed for the night, and breakfast. We have also left you a great review.

❤️ There were no cobbles today.

❤️ Tony bought a new pair of trainers and his feet are very grateful (although the budget is now blown).

❤️ It was surprisingly nice walking in the warm rain.

❤️ The part of the trail by the river was truly beautiful.

❤️ We met a crazy pair of Spanish ladies, wearing bin bags as rain coats, who made us laugh.

❤️ No new blisters for either of us!

❤️ We had a lovely pilgrim meal at **Restaurante O Carreteiro** in Porriño: 2 courses plus wine and coffee for just €12.50 - and they gave us extra wine for **free!**

❤️ We found a supermarket and could buy shampoo, wine and chocolate.

❤️ We found an albergue with beds (and we are not going out tonight) 🤣

❤️ Only 100 kilometres to go to Santiago de Compostela.

❤️ At 6pm the sun came out 🌞 so we had a glass of wine outside to celebrate all the things we have to be thankful for 🥂

Today, for the first time, we were walking in Spain, and began by walking through the historic town of Tui, famous for its cathedral-fort. Once out of the town, we had a choice to make; there were two routes to O Porriño, the direct route along paths and roads and through an industrial estate, or an alternative through the 'As Gándaras de Budiño' nature reserve and following the River Louro which was a couple of kilometres further.

We chose the latter, and followed a very pretty, but muddy, path which followed the river faithfully for eight kilometres. We were rewarded by meandering paths, the twitter of birdsong, pools of emerald water, gentle waterfalls and the pitter-patter of gentle rain on the canopy overhead, much nicer than an industrial estate.

After yet another fabulous lunch, this time in O Porriño, we decided to continue to Mós, which we had identified as our next overnight stop. As we walked, however, the rain got heavier and heavier, until we were soaked through, despite our waterproofs. We sheltered under a large oak tree to refer to the route map, and decided to cut today's leg short. We had seen a lot of people walking today, The Way seeming to be much busier in Spain than in it had been in Portugal, and we were worried that if we continued to Mós, the albergues would be full and we would then have to make a decision – to continue to Pontevedra or come back to Veigadaña. We didn't want to carry on to Pontevedra, several more miles in the rain, and it seemed pointless risking having to retrace our steps tomorrow, so we stopped at a hostel and settled in for the night.

The dormitory was steaming, as wet clothes were draped over every available chair – the airers being full to capacity and the heaters turned on high. But at least we had a bed for the night.

Day 7: the power of positive thought

Ponte da Veiga do Louro, on the outskirts of Tui, where a stone pilgrim stands guard.

100 kilometres to go! A landmark moment.

As Gándaras de Budiño nature reserve following the River Louro.

Chapter 17

Canadians

Before starting our Camino, we stayed overnight at the Sandeman's hostel in Porto, a fabulous place to stay, and somewhere I would be happy to recommend to anyone. The great thing about hostels is that you tend to meet interesting people – people with great stories – so, after a restful night in the 'Squid Game' style dormitory, we made our way to the communal living area, for breakfast and some more people-watching. We had spent an hour the previous evening trying to guess where people had travelled from and what their stories were: one man, a lone traveller, looked just like Vladimir Putin and we entertained ourselves by developing a fictional scenario to explain why he was here; he could be plotting against Portugal! Should we call the authorities?

In the light of a new morning, our imaginations were not running quite as wildly, and we sat ourself down at the huge, refectory-style, breakfast table. After enjoying a feast of scrambled eggs, croissants and fruit, we were discussing our plans for the day over coffee, when a lady plonked herself down on a chair opposite with a frustrated sigh. She immediately started talking, and introduced her nationality as Canadian. She obviously had a lot on her mind and needed to unload, as she then talked for about half an hour, barely coming up for air, as she told us about her frustrating journey the previous day. She had travelled alone from her home in Toronto, and was meeting her friend in Porto to walk the Portuguese Way. Her plan had been to have a day by herself first, seeing the sights, but her flight had been delayed. She had spent twelve hours in the airport, missed her transfer and then had to argue her case with the car hire company, who wanted to charge her extra for changing her agreement dates. After a long argument, which she had won, she had then lost the keys of her hire car and had to go back to the company to beg for their help - all before getting to the hostel. Arriving late, she had to access her bed in the dorm' in the dark, and had almost selected the wrong one, just realising her mistake before climbing in next to a complete stranger; she had had a bad day and then a bad night and just needed to tell someone. I was glad we could be there for her, and hope she met up with her friend and enjoyed her Camino without any further incidents.

The next Canadian we chatted to was another lady who was staying at the same hostel as us on our first night. We were staying at a monastery which did have kitchen facilities, but unfortunately, we had no food with us so we had been given directions to a restaurant about a kilometre away. We hobbled downhill to the restaurant and enjoyed our first experience of a pilgrim meal: vegetable soup with a bread roll, chicken, rice and vegetables, a slice of the local cake and a glass of wine. As we ate, we watched as more and more walkers were seated, all hungrily devouring the same simple food.

We left the restaurant at the same time as the Canadian lady, and on the walk back up the hill to the monastery, she told us about her pilgrimage. She had spent the last three and a half weeks walking; the first two weeks she had walked from Porto to Santiago de Compostela, with her parents ages seventy and seventy-two! They had all completed the walk, and she was now on her way back to Porto to meet up with some friends, having walked all the way back again in just six days. Her parents had picked up a car and were now driving down through Portugal, visiting some bucket-list places on the way, before spending a week in the Algarve and then returning to Canada. Good for them! I hope that I am still having amazing adventures when I'm in my seventies.

Whilst walking to Pontevedra, we met Bella, who was completing her first Camino at only eight months old. She was travelling in a specially adapted pram, with her Canadian Mum and Nan taking turns to push the pram; her mum had completed the walk once before, eight years ago with friends, but her nan said she rarely walked anywhere so this was a huge challenge for her. Bella had been born prematurely with several health problems as a result, and it sounded as though they had all had a difficult time since her birth. However, as some of her problems had resolved as she had grown, the doctors had given them the green light to travel. No relaxing beach holiday for these ladies though, they had chosen to walk the Portuguese Way – huge respect to them!

I asked about their experience so far, and they said that they had been overwhelmed by people's kindness. Most parts of the trail are rural – muddy, rocky, hilly – and those cobblestones! – but they had managed with help of their fellow walkers. People had helped to push, lift and manoeuvre the pram over obstacles and along difficult stretches, and without exception, walkers had offered moral support and encouragement unwaveringly.

Our paths crossed another couple times before we lost touch; once in a restaurant where we had a giggle over the strange food we had ordered – none of us understanding the menu. And another time when we were traversing the 'mountain' on the way to *Rubiães,* where we witnessed first-hand, four young men carrying the pram up the mountain. A great example of that Camino spirit and camaraderie.

So, lots of Canadians walking The Way, all with their own reasons and stories, and all inspirational in their own way.

Chapter 18

Day 8 – Everybody should walk a Camino

Veigadaña to Arcade

Distance walked: 21 kilometres

Everybody should walk at least one Camino in their life. Yes everyone! - and the younger the better, like a kind of national service. I can't believe it has taken us this long to get round to it - we have been talking about it for the last ten years!

I don't say this because it's easy (it isn't) or because it's hard, which goes without saying, but because it teaches you (or reminds you) about what is important in life; kindness, helping each other, perseverance, perspective, patience, resilience...

It is wonderful to engage with people, young and old, of all nationalities and faiths; to know that they will almost certainly help or support you if you need a chat, a blister plaster or indeed, anything else.

These are people who love and respect the countryside; there is no litter or damage anywhere, and albergue dormitories, bathrooms and kitchens are left as they are found. People living side by side, despite their everyday differences; enjoying each other's company and being the best versions of themselves.

I haven't quite come to the point of epiphany, but walking for six hours a day does give you a lot of thinking time, and has allowed me to draw a few early conclusions, in fact, more than a few.

I am beginning to see that walking a camino is a bit like living a whole life compressed into a fortnight: there are the same highs and lows, the same range of emotions felt and plenty of physical obstacles to overcome, which are only intensified by being compressed into such a short space of time. It's an emotional rollercoaster and some parts are better than others;

at night you can go to bed feeling that you won't be able to face another walk tomorrow, and then the next morning, inexplicably, life seems full of possibility once again.

Today we walked from Veigadaña to Arcade, about another twenty-one kilometres and taking our camino total to about one hundred and seventy kilometres - an incredible achievement!

We walked out of town, about a kilometre through the old winding streets, before turning left onto the Camino de Esteiro where the trail became more rural.

We had noticed a large increase in the number of people walking since we left Tui yesterday, and today there seemed to be almost a queue lining the narrow dirt path. However, as the morning continued, the throng thinned out and we regained our space, walking first through vineyards and then beneath trees, before climbing up through the forest where there were beautiful views of the valley.

We stopped at a roadside cafe bar for breakfast, sharing a delicious tortilla, then continued uphill, along roads and pathways, past an old fountain and picnic area, and a little later, a stone wall where there is yet another wonderful tribute to pilgrims. We paused for a moment, marvelling at the crazy range of memorabilia on display, then continued, this time steeply downhill – the first hill of the day conquered.

Further along the trail, around lunchtime, we stopped for a drink and some 'complementary' tapas in Redondela, before tackling the second hill, this time ascending through the fragrant aroma of the eucalyptus trees. We almost took a wrong turn at a new marker, but after deliberation with some other pelegrinos, we continued along the track and reached the peak of the hill to be rewarded by our first view of the coast since Porto; a grand view of the Ria de Vigo. From here we had another steep descent down a dirt path passing a fountain on the right with an iron sculpture of a pilgrim family set playfully in front of it.

From this point, we had to walk along the busy N-550 highway into Arcade which lacked the aesthetics of the scenery we had been enjoying, but seemed to be the only route available. Reaching a fork in the road, we took the right turn, passing another pilgrim tribute before arriving at our albergue for the night.

Another good day on our journey of self-discovery.

Day 8: everybody should walk a camino

Many more people joined the Portuguese Way once we reached Spain, as lots of pilgrims choose to walk the last 100 kilometres, from Tui to Santiago de Compostela.

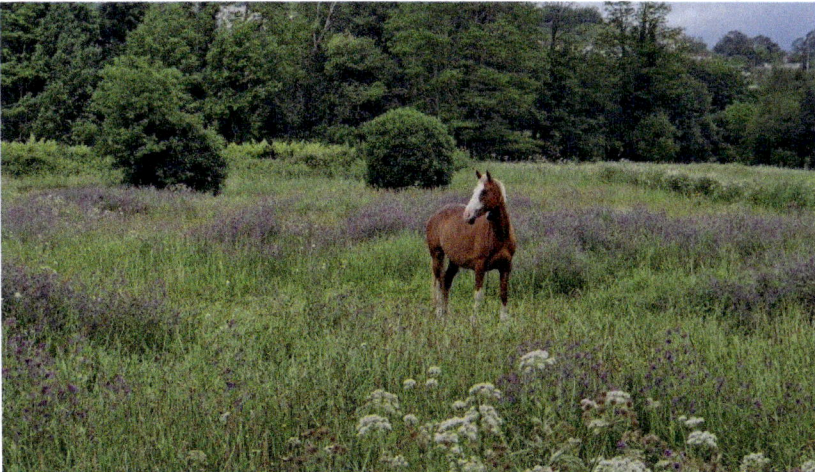

Chapter 19

Martin

Martin was one of those people that you don't come across very often. He seemed to be a lone walker, and although we had crossed each other's path a couple of times, we had never exchanged more than a polite good morning; sometimes he was chatting with another walker, or in a group, but more often he was walking alone, quite contentedly, in front of us or behind us. This particular day, in our first week of walking, we had stopped at a small café. According to the map there were few stopping points today, and it was hot! The sun was beating down already and the café was busy with walkers: chatting, drinking coffee, filling up their water bottles and stocking up on snacks for the next part of the journey, a long valley-walk amidst vineyards.

It just so happened that we left the café at the same time as Martin and fell into step. After introductions, he told us a little about himself. He was originally from Armenia, but had moved to London ten years ago to find work. He was now working as a hairdresser, a job he loved, and had made a home with his partner in the city. He said he liked the hustle and bustle of London, but did feel the need to escape occasionally. Walking was his escape. His solitude. He was a pleasant young man, asking about our lives and our reasons for walking, and he was very vocal about his love of the countryside we were walking through and the sense of peace it brought him.

We had been walking companionably for a while, when my husband asked Martin his reason for walking a pilgrimage, and whether his reasons were religious or spiritual. This may sound like a very personal question, but it is actually a common theme of conversation on the Camino and one that is more often than not discussed with everyone you walk or talk with. Even 'not having a reason' is usually unpicked and a tenuous reason discovered, often personal, and sometimes not open for discussion, as sometimes a person's conversation needs to be within their own head if they are trying to figure out a problem or make a difficult decision about something.

Martin talked very freely about his own reason for walking, and despite not raising it himself, I got the feeling that he had shared his story many times. He told us that several years ago he had been diagnosed with skin cancer and he pointed to several scars on his legs where the lesions had been. He talked in detail about his experience of the process of diagnosis and treatment, speaking highly of the national health service in the UK (something that he would not have had access to in his own country) and the professionals involved in his care. He had treatment for two years before finally going into remission and beginning to rebuild his life.

He said that he loved his job as a hairdresser, and enjoyed the interaction with people; in fact, he had met his partner through his work and they were very happy together. He said that his illness had made him appreciate his life and his health and that during his time recovering, he had enjoyed long walks in the parks and open spaces near where he lived.

It was then that he dropped the bombshell – the cancer was back and it had spread.

I was floored and found myself floundering for any words that I could have used that would even begin to express understanding, or to say what was needed; words of comfort seemed inadequate somehow, and how could you offer words of optimism for someone who was going through something so horrific for the second time in his young life – it seemed so cruel.

Despite his situation, Martin was very pragmatic about his situation and positive about his uncertain future. Following the latest raft of tests, his doctor had given his blessing for this trip and encouraged him to immerse himself in the experience. He knew what lay ahead of him when he returned to London, and he hoped to face his latest challenge with an inner strength that he believed he would gain from his reflections on The Way. He was certainly resolute that he would enjoy whatever time he had left in this world, and that however long or short, life was a gift that we should all live to the full.

You may think that this interaction would have left us deflated and a little sad for Martin and his awful situation, but it actually left us full of admiration for this brave young man who was accepting of his fate and had resolved to give himself time to walk, in meditation, to gain the strength he knew he would need. There was no edge of bitterness about him, and no self-pity, and for me, that made him heroic and a positive role model for all. I certainly think of him often, and pray that his treatment went well.

Chapter 20

Day 9 – Sauntering through Sunshine and Showers

Arcade to Pontevedra

Distance walked: 12 kilometres

A short stretch today, only twelve kilometres on the 'Way', and there was definitely a 'water' theme, with the walk punctuated by heavy showers and only a few brief sunny spells. We left Arcade, crossing the Rio Verdugo by traversing the Medieval Pontesampaio, yet another magnificent medieval stone-arched bridge, one hundred and forty-four metres in length. Historically, anybody crossing this bridge had to pay a toll, but thanks to the archbishop of Santiago de Compostela, this practice ended in the 12th century, giving pilgrims freedom to cross, a kindness now extended to everyone.

It was raining as we crossed the river and started to climb through the narrow, cobbled streets, and as the showers became heavier, we found ourselves dodging under porches for shelter and standing in doorways to avoid the worst of it. We didn't want to invite the same fate as one young lady who stayed at the same albergue as us last night: after walking almost forty kilometres in the rain, she arrived with soaked boots and feet full of blisters, a nightmare we were keen to avoid.

As we sheltered under a small porch, the door opened and the lady who lived there came out to usher us inside until the rain lightened, chatting away to us in Spanish about the rain - *'mucho agua'* - and her daughter who moved to Seattle to get away from the rain, only to find that Seattle is also a rainy place, which made the lady roar with laughter. She said a lot more, very little of which we understood, and eventually waved us off with her good wishes when the rain abated. What a lovely lady!

Half an hour later, the rain had stopped and the sun was shining from a blue sky, a pattern that was to be repeated for the next few hours, our raincoats on and then off and then on again, sheltering from the rain under trees where we could and rejoicing in the warmth when the sun did peep out from behind the clouds. The walk itself was lovely, the first couple of hours through fields of vines beside a quietly flowing river. There were a few steep sections as we approached the woods, and then a long stretch without any watering holes, so by the time we reached the outskirts of Pontevedra we were ready for a well-earned coffee and a bite to eat.

We were certainly not alone today, there were many people walking, some alone, others as couples like us, and also some quite big groups, which has been more typical since Tui.

As we approached Pontevedra, we had the option of continuing along the road or walking by the river and taking a slightly longer route. We chose to walk by the river as it seemed quieter, enjoying the meandering water, which eddied and flowed beside the path. We found ourselves immersed in vibrant greenery with splashes of colour from the native wildflowers; a woodland blanket of emerald ferns, pretty tri-petalled white flowers of the Wandering-Jew, yellow Celandine, creeping Forget-me-not and the frilly white blooms of Giant Hogweed.

As we **sauntered*** along the quiet muddy path, with the pitter-patter of rain just breaking through the canopy of the trees, I could almost have been back in Lancashire, walking through an English woodland; only the smell of eucalyptus was different. We emerged from the trees to rejoin the main path running alongside the road into Pontevedra - city of bridges. The old town is beautiful, its narrow streets full of traditional stone buildings adorned with brightly-coloured pots and baskets of vibrant flowers. There is plenty to see: churches, convents and statues, but if you only see one thing, make it the Santuario de la Virgen Peregrina de Pontevedra (sanctuary of the virgin pilgrim), built in the baroque style with a floor plan in the shape of a scallop shell; it is very impressive and very fitting. Having dropped our bags at the City Hostel and rested awhile, we made our way down to the river, to wander along the old streets, enjoy a nice bottle of wine and some good food, and to celebrate our sauntering.

*saunter Isn't it a beautiful word. Back in the Middle Ages people used to go on pilgrimages to the Holy Land, and when people in the villages through which they passed asked where they were going, they would reply, 'A la sainte terre.' 'To the Holy Land.' And so, they became known as sainte-terre-ers or saunterers.

Day 9: sauntering through sunshine and showers to beautiful Pontevedra

Beautiful architecture and
delicious pilgrim plates
In Pontevedra

Chapter 21

Rolf

It was a hot day and it had been a long walk. We were sat in a tiny strip of shade in front of the only café in the village, trying to muster up the strength to tackle the four-kilometre-long hill that was in front of us. We knew that once we had climbed it, we were home and dry, for the hostel we were planning to stay at was not much further, but still we were not looking forward to the hill, looming ahead of us in the heat of the day like some sort of monster.

As we avoided the inevitable, by sipping our drinks as slowly as possible, a man approached. He looked exhausted, bent over under the weight of his backpack and sweating profusely. In one fluid movement, he shed his backpack, dumped it on the ground and crashed to a halt into one of the plastic chairs, leaning back and groaning loudly, clearly oblivious of us sitting right in front of him. When he had caught his breath and regained some of his composure, we introduced ourselves and asked if he was ok. He told us that he had been walking for over forty kilometres, having walked all the way from Porto to Portela de Tamel in one day, a journey that we had undertaken in three. He had started off on the coastal route before changing his mind and heading inland, and the distance hadn't phased him - but he hadn't taken into account the heat of the day. "I can't climb that hill!" he exclaimed, still breathing hard and waving his hand in the direction of the road ahead, "I've done it before and I know what it's like. I just can't face it."

He introduced himself as Rolf. He was German and walking alone, as he had done for the past six years. He later told us that his two-weeks walking the Portuguese Way gave him and his wife a break from each other, time to miss each other, as he put it; time when they each did their own thing – and he had come to look forward to some time alone for reflection; to forget about everything else and just enjoy the walk. It would appear, however, that today he had bit off more than he could chew, and was now too tired to finish the last few kilometres.

"Do you want me to get you a taxi?" Tony asked, realising that this wasn't just bluster; he

73

really didn't want to walk any further. Rolf laughed and said that if we could get him one, he would be very grateful. The way he laughed before speaking, indicated that he thought it was unlikely that we would have either the phone signal or the good fortune, to actually get hold of a taxi; after all we were in a tiny village in the middle of the Portuguese countryside, surrounded by hills. But we were in luck – he was in luck, and within ten minutes an Uber pulled up outside the café. We bundled Rolf inside and sent him on his way, telling him to get the beers in for when we arrived.

He was true to his word and bought the beers all evening, 'a fair exchange' he said, for not having to climb that hill. Over pizza, he told us that he worked in car manufacturing in his home town, and that cars were his passion. His other passion were his dogs, which he walked for miles every day. He and Tony had a lot to talk about, as Tony had also worked in car manufacturing, and they enjoyed exchanging stories, putting forward their different opinions about the best and worst car brands, and generally putting the 'car production' world to rights, before we turned in for the night.

The next day was the leg to Ponta de Lima, but we didn't walk with Rolf; he was an early riser and would have been half way there before we even hit the road. By the time we arrived, with blistered feet and aching backs, all we wanted to do was lie on our bunks until everything stopped hurting.

Later, Rolf sought us out and asked if we would like to go into the town for something to eat, but 'Town' meant back over the bridge, and I really couldn't face it. We said that we wanted to stay close to the hostel, and although we did wander the streets for a while together looking for somewhere to eat, he gave up before us, trotting back across the bridge that for me had become a symbol of pain, and we never saw him again. That's just the way it is on the Camino, acquaintances come and go, each adding a little more colour to the day and another story to your portfolio.

Chapter 22

Day 10 – Suffering

Pontevedra to Caldas de Reis

Distance walked: 23 kilometres

Today's walk took us out of Pontevedra over another historic bridge, the Puente del Burgo, a medieval bridge on the site of an even earlier roman construction. Just out of town, we reached a fork in the path, a well-documented point on the Portuguese Way, where an alternative route can be taken.

The Spiritual Route – or *Variante Espiritual* – heads back towards the Atlantic, following the journey made by the remains of the apostle James, from Jerusalem to Iria Flavia and then on to Santiago. It adds a couple of days to the central route, that we are walking, but is reported to add stunning countryside, beautiful coastal views and a boat ride from Vilanova de Arousa to Pontecesures – maybe next time.

Following the central route as planned, the route was gentle and flat, passing through several small settlements, each with its own pilgrim chapel. The path then continued along the valley under huge oak trees – an idyllic natural spot and full of birdsong. A couple of hours later, we crossed a railway line to enter Barro, and continued through Tivo until we reached Caldas de Reis, an iconic town on The Way that is frequently visited for the alleged medical properties of its thermal waters. We also discovered that there is an additional nine-kilometre circular route from the centre of the town, where you can see several waterfalls in a stunning natural environment, including the Cascades of the Barosa River, which we had missed on the way into town. After walking seventeen miles, we weren't up to another walk today, however spectacular, but it's yet another reason to return.

For just two weeks we are pilgrims, travelling on foot from Porto to Santiago de Compostela, a total of two hundred and forty-eight kilometres and not a journey that I ever thought would be easy. Our reason for walking? I am not sure that I can define a reason; there is definitely a cultural and historical element; the Way of St James is a legendary pilgrimage, rich in medieval alure. The route itself has been recognised as a UNESCO world heritage site and is in itself, a journey through history.

I was also attracted to the idea of an unforgettable adventure; something we could do together whilst meeting other adventurous souls from all over the world, and hearing their stories. I think the final reason was probably just to see if I could do it - to walk day after day, immersed in nature, and to see where my thoughts would take me – and although for me, it was not a journey taken for religious reasons, there is no denying the spiritual side of it (something I feel wherever I walk) and I was prepared to embrace whatever I faced head on.

One thing that we have faced from the very beginning is suffering: aching feet at the end of every day on the path, an aching back and sore shoulders from carrying a heavy backpack, uncertainty about whether we would find somewhere to stay every night, discomfort when that shelter turned out to be a narrow, hard mattress with a scratchy woollen blanket, and variable weather conditions which have ranged from the hot sun beating down on us day after day in the first week, to plummeting temperatures and the pouring rain in the second week.

Blisters have been a big problem for both of us; the weight of a backpack combined with the cobbled and rough stones of the Portuguese route having a massive impact on our feet. We have become 'adept' at binding and plastering our feet each morning, and checking for new damage each night. Some days in the first week, on reaching our destination we struggled to imagine that we would be able to continue the next morning - but despite the difficulties, we always did.

For us, we would reach Caldas de Reis on day ten. Ten days of walking, and the day we would hit the magical two-hundred-kilometre mark, leaving only forty-eight kilometres to go until we would reach Santiago de Compostela. There was no longer any doubt at all that we would make it.

We had twenty-four kilometres to walk, one of our longer stretches, and after ten kilometres my toe started to hurt - a recurrence of my first injury, a huge blister on my little toe. We stopped and I re-strapped the toe, improving it slightly, but then my knee began to hurt as well, probably because I had altered my gait. As if that wasn't enough, I was suffering from some chaffing - this was not good, there was still at least ten kilometres to go.

I hobbled on for a few kilometres until we reached a rest spot and we stopped for a drink.

I had another fiddle with my plasters, applied some Vaseline and took a couple of painkillers, and half an hour later we rejoined the path. Chaffing alleviated and toe well-strapped, the knee seemed to sort itself out, and a couple of hours later we arrived re-energised in Caldas de Reis.

It's tough being a pilgrim; the struggle is real and the suffering is sometimes hard to overcome. But I have no doubt that after a good meal and a good night's rest, we will be ready to do it all again tomorrow.

Here are some words that I felt that I needed to define after today's walk:

Pilgrim - (noun) - *definition*: one who journeys in a foreign land; often to a sacred place for religious or cultural reasons.

Pilgrimage - (noun) - *definition*: to go on a prolonged journey, often undertaken on foot or on horseback, toward a specific destination of significance.

Suffering - *(noun)* - *definition*: the state of undergoing pain, distress, or hardship.

To struggle - (verb) - definition: to make strenuous efforts in the face of difficulties

And some quotes that seemed particularly fitting:

Christians are encouraged to see themselves as 'pilgrims and strangers on the earth', 'temporary residents' whose true home is in heaven. *(1ˢᵗ epistle of Peter 2:11; Hebrews 11:13)*.

The harder the struggle, the more glorious the triumph. Self-realisation demands very great struggle. *Swami Sivananda*

After climbing a great hill, one only finds that there are many more hills to climb. *Nelson Mandela*

We are all pilgrims…our life Is a long walk from Earth to Heaven. *Vincent van Gogh*

It would seem that we are all in agreement. Here's to all our future hills and struggles.

Buen Camino!

Day 10: suffering

The healing springs at Caldas de Reis (above), and the Cascades of the Barosa River (below)

Chapter 23

Brazilians

I have already mentioned the Brazilian walkers, but feel that they walked alongside us, more-or-less for the duration of our Camino, and as such became 'fellow-walkers' and deserve a chapter of their own.

The first time I saw them was in the queue at the Cathedral in Porto, waiting for our Pilgrim Passports, and we had exchanged tentative hellos, as we did with many walkers that day. The second time our paths crossed was at the Pedra Furada hostel at the end of our second day. We were hot and tired when we arrived, and flopped ourselves down on a couple of plastic chairs in the garden. Felipe and Eliana were sat opposite in their own pair of matching chairs looking equally exhausted, and we exchanged a celebratory wave, congratulating each other on surviving another day. Not being brave enough to challenge the language barrier, we did not speak to each other but did share a couple of comedic moments: the first when Eliana was collecting in some clothes she had washed and was caught up in a tangle of underwear, and the second when an unsuspecting Tony was suddenly drenched by the onset of the sprinkler system – a much needed but unexpected cool down after a very hot day on the trail.

A couple of days later, as I described earlier, we were resting in the shade outside a café. Along came Felipe and Eliana, waving as they passed us, and then a few moments later we were joined by Rolf, whose story I have already told. Once Rolf had been dispatched to the hostel in his taxi, we set off to tackle the notorious 'hill', four miles of steep ascent in the blistering heat. I was not looking forward to it; it was the end of the day's section and we were hot and tired, and we were both beginning to feel seriously impeded by the blisters on our feet. It was going to feel like we were walking on coals up that hill and I was questioning my decision not to share the taxi with Rolf.

As the road began to climb, we came across Felipe and his mum sitting on a wall. Eliana had taken her trainers off and they both looked how we felt – broken. We stopped to ask if we could help, although we knew this was unlikely, and somehow managed to communicate our mutual understanding and sympathy without words.

At this point, we didn't know that they were Brazilian, and it was only when I heard Felipe ask his mum if she could continue, that I realised he was speaking Portuguese. Knowing a little Portuguese myself, I asked where they were from, and from there struck up a stilted conversation with Felipe, who could speak a little English. With the help of google translate, and a lot of effort and miming, we learned about their life in Brazil, and they of ours in England. Felipe was an engineer and was learning to speak English as he wanted to travel. His mum spoke no English at all and had lived in Brazil all her life, but was a teacher like me, so we had something in common and she appreciated my attempts to speak with her in Portuguese. Felipe showed us whereabouts in Brazil they lived, and told us about the terrible floods that had ravaged their town and the surrounding areas in the previous months. They were not seasoned walkers, but had decided that they wanted to do something together; Eliana had always wanted to walk a Camino and, as they spoke the language, the Portuguese Way seemed the obvious choice.

We completed the climb together, made easier by the distraction and mental gymnastics involved in communicating, and by the time we arrived at the night's accommodation, we were friends and assured each other that we would be welcome, should travel bring us to each other's doors, in either Brazil or England.

The next time we met was in Tui, when we had crossed the border into Spain. After checking in, we trudged up two flights of stairs to the dormitory, where they were already resting on their bunks. We waved a hello, and checked in on each other about the blisters, but didn't see them again because of our 'lockout' situation that followed. When we caught up with them later in the journey, Felipe was horrified at the story we told about being locked out, as he said that he had thought he heard banging, and now regretted that he hadn't investigated. What a shame we hadn't exchanged phone numbers, he could have come down and let us in which would have solved a huge problem – although it would have been one less story to tell.

We didn't meet up again until Santiago, where once again, we met in the queue at the cathedral awaiting our Compostela. This time we did exchange phone numbers and now keep up with each other's travels on Instagram.

Chapter 24

Day 11 – Padrón. The birth of a Legend and The Way

Caldas de Reis to Padrón

Distance walked: 25 kilometres

The trail from Caldas de Reis to Padrón took us along roads and dirt trails, through woods and through tiny hamlets and often surrounded by the very 'Portuguese' smell of Eucalyptus. We travel to Madeira often, and the very first, and nicest, thing that I notice whenever we get out of the car in Sao Vicente, is the wonderful scent of Eucalyptus, omnipresent and welcoming.

Caldas de Reis is famous for its thermal springs, and after soaking our worn-out feet in the healing waters, we set out along the Bermana Valley, walking between fields of crops and passing the beautiful church of Santa Maria de Carracedo and its ruined monastery. We had hoped to see its chapels of San Diego and Del Carmen dating from the seventeenth and eighteenth centuries, but sadly the doors were locked so we rejoined the footpath and followed the route through a dense forest along the River Valga. It was a gentle route, dappled by sunlight filtering through the trees and passing several pilgrim shrines, all colourfully decorated with lengths of ribbon, flags and other memorabilia, each one urging us forward towards Santiago de Compostela.

Beneath the trees, the path undulated pleasantly, constantly changing from soil to stone, from rocky slabs to a leaf-littered forest floor, and as well as nature's carpet underfoot we were accompanied by the meditative tones of its song – the drip, drip of last night's rain from the trees and the whispering voice of the river encouraging us on our way.

Out of the forest and ignoring the rare grey ugliness of the city suburbs, we crossed a bridge over the River Ulla and walked along its banks into the centre of Padrón, where we were greeted by the unusual rows of monumental Plátano trees in the central square, the Padrón

Alameda. Across another bridge, this one spanning the River Sar, we found ourselves at the Hostel, the traditional first albergue of Padrón, containing just one dormitory with forty-eight beds, a large kitchen and shower rooms. With the sun making a rare appearance, we showered quickly and left our bags on our beds, before setting off to explore this small but beautiful city, a place that I had looked forward to seeing since reading about the walk.

But Padrón is not just another town on the Portuguese Way - it's importance to pilgrims is upheld by the story of St James, whose body was transported, by boat, to the nearby estuary of the Ulla and Sar rivers near Iria Flavia. The apostle James was beheaded by King Herod as part of the Judean king's persecution against the early Christians in the 1st century AD, and after being brought to Galicia by boat, the body is said to have been transferred onto land via a stone altar slab, or 'padrón'. This altar is what gives the present town of Padrón its name, and the legend is supported by evidence – the existence of an altar, which has been preserved and can be seen in the parish church of Santiago de Padrón. Thus, Padrón is recognised as the starting point of St James' final journey and the overland transfer of his body to Compostela, a pilgrimage that is celebrated locally every 25th July, and daily by the pilgrims that pass through on their way to Santiago.

Today, Padrón is a lovely old town, full of attractive plazas containing statues celebrating local people who have left their mark on the community. In each of these squares are little restaurants and cafes, including the one I described earlier in chapter 12, all selling the famous Padrón Peppers amongst other local delicacies. There were also many beautiful medieval buildings, churches and museums, most of which had sadly closed by the time we arrived; it is a delightful rabbit warren of a place, connected by its faith, its many bridges and the water that runs beneath them, and as the sun set, we watched from a table at a small bar in the narrowest of streets and enjoyed a glass of cold wine serenaded by the ever-constant sound of water reaching out to us, as we contemplated the final days of our own pilgrimage.

Day 11: Padrón

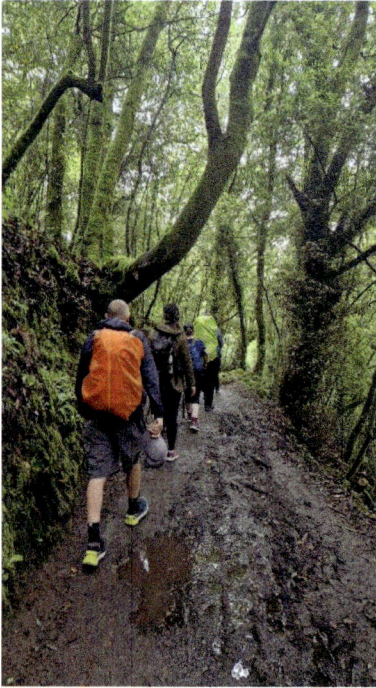

The final march Into Padrón   Another pilgrim way marker

And below, the beautiful Padrón Alameda with Its rows of magnificent platano trees.

Chapter 25

Everybody has a Story

One of the most interesting things about this experience has been meeting people along the way. Although most people are travelling in groups, and offer no more than a "Buen Camino" as they pass you, some you walk alongside for a while and get to hear a little of their story – and it seems that everybody has a story.

One thing I have tried to be better at, over the course of the walk, is listening. I don't think I am a great listener; I tend to chatter away when I meet new people, maybe because I'm nervous or because the silence can be uncomfortable, I don't really know why.

But then it occurred to me, that if you tell everyone you meet your story, or even a small part of it, then that is the only thing you hear, and you learn nothing new.

So I have been listening: to people who I have met along the way, to my own inner voice, to the sounds of nature; trying to listen without opinion, judgement or comment and to see what I can learn, or what I can give - just by being present.

I have already written about some of the people we made connections with, from Canada, Australia, Brazil; and there were many others from all over Europe and beyond, many whom we never even exchanged names with, such is the transient nature of life on the road.

Whilst walking through Portugal, we met an Asian couple who were very political and keen to discuss the current difficulties between Israel and Hamas. We had heard their lively debate some days earlier in a hostel, and now spent a lively hour at a café listening to another discussion between them and a larger group of walkers, all hailing from different places around the world, and all keen to have their say.

Wendy and Mary were friends from California, walking together. Mary was a teacher, so we had a lot to talk about. But Wendy's story was far more interesting; she had lost a friend who had been attacked by a wildcat whilst out hiking, and she had also lost her home and everything in it, during one of the recent wild fires in California. Despite this, she was thankful for the opportunity this walk was giving her; to spend time with her friend in the beautiful Portuguese countryside and for the space and time to plan the next stage of her life. Most of all, she said that she was just thankful to be alive.

Several times we crossed paths with 'The Portuguese Kids', a trio - two boys and a girl - who were very positive and upbeat, walking in deck shoes and shorts with the smallest of backpacks, and not even a hint of a blister between them. They were lively and very friendly, enjoying the company of anyone they came across and totally immersing themselves in their Camino experience with the carefree attitude of youth. I remember one night when they were staying at the same hostel as us and returned from an evening out more than a little merry. They were still up and gone the next morning by the time we were rising.

I had a brief encounter with Josef, another walker from Brazil. We had an impromptu half-hour encounter whilst waiting at the reception desk of the at one of the hostels. He noticed the plasters on my feet, and after asking how I was managing them, he gave me a small tube of blister cream – the one he swore by. To return the favour, I invited him to share the only free washing machine as I only had half a load. The blister cream wasn't quite the miracle cure that he promised, but it was a very kind gesture and typical of the generosity of most of the people we met.

In Pontevedra, we met Bella for the first time; eight months old and completing the camino with her Canadian mum and nan. We ran into each other again in a restaurant a couple of days later. It was the end of the day and we were looking at the menu, when the waiter asked us to move to a different table and started to rearrange the remaining tables around us. He was making a space for them to come and sit with Bella's pram alongside them.

Together, we perused the menu; it seemed to be tapas, but most of it was undecipherable, the names of the dishes so unusual and unfamiliar that even google was non-plussed. The prices were cheap, so we took it at face value and ordered all eight dishes on the menu, expecting small plates. We were wrong. They were quite large plates and we were very, very full by the time we had attempted to eat it all. Bella's mum and nan enjoyed a laugh at our expense, and learning from our mistake, ordered much more sensibly. As with others, our paths continued to cross for several days before we lost touch, but what a lovely family.

We met China Man in Veigadaña. He was in the next bunk in a hostel with very few power points. There were none next to our bunks so he let us use his super-duper power pack to charge our phones. We met again the next night at the albergue and a couple of other times at cafes over the next day or two. We never actually spoke to each other, but always exchanged a friendly smile and a wave.

Once we crossed to Spain, Interactions became less frequent. It seemed that most people were travelling in large groups and their luggage was being transported for them. They all seemed to know each other and seemed less fatigued than us, probably because they hadn't walked as far and weren't carrying a large backpack, so it was a quick "Buen Camino" and off they went.

One group we did criss-cross with for a couple of days was a large assisted group. The first time we saw them ahead of us we were quite irritated; we had become used to the calm tranquility on the trail, and with this group there was a lot of noisy laughing and shouting, and quite a bit of horseplay. As we got nearer, however, we realised that they were a group of thirty or forty young adults with a range of disabilities, just enjoying the camaraderie of each other's company, laughing and singing. Our irritation evaporated, to be replaced with a huge respect for both them and their carers. What an experience for them to be having! They were definitely the most upbeat group we met and always had a friendly "Buen Camino" for us whenever we passed each other.

We even met a group from Halifax - I recognised the Yorkshire accent straight away. They were two couples on holiday together in Portugal, and were on a day walk to Valinhas. We enjoyed a lovely exchange about Halifax and Clitheroe and they told us about some of their favourite walking routes on the East Yorkshire Coast. It's a small world!

Finally, after our final full day's walking, we met a whole group of people, including two lovely guys from Ireland, Glenn and Julian. More about that in the next chapter.

Chapter 26

Day 12 – Delaying the end

Padrón to Lugar de Pedreira

Distance walked: 14 kilometres

Today was our last full day's walking before we hoped to reach Santiago de Compostela, and the end of our pilgrimage. Two weeks of just putting one foot in front of the other; two weeks of carrying on despite the aches and pains accumulated on the way; two weeks of beautiful Portuguese and Galician countryside, of sunshine and rainfall, of the almost constant sound of running water from the streams and waterfalls, ancient pathways, churches and bridges, and two weeks of walking alongside lovely people from all over the world. Indeed, today we were reunited on the trail with Wendy and Mary, and also with Felipe and his mum Eliana, all of whom we met right back at the beginning in Portugal.

With only twenty-five kilometres left between Padrón and Santiago, at a push, we could have completed the last stage in one day, most people do. However, for a few reasons, we decided to split it into two parts, walking to Lugar de Pedreira today and leaving the grand finale for tomorrow, when we hoped to arrive as the midday bells were ringing out at the cathedral.

One of the reasons to compete in two smaller stretches was that I had picked up an injury. I had strained my iliotibial band – a long length of connective tissue running from the thigh down to the shin bone – and it was causing me a great deal of discomfort on the outer side of my left knee; I could have predicted that my knee would bother me, but I hadn't thought it would be a cartilage problem. Another reason was just to extend the walk; after struggling so much with blisters at the start, we were now really enjoying the day-on-day experience and actually didn't want it to end. The final reason was simply that we had time, with another few nights remaining until our prebooked flights home. We had allowed for rest and injury days and had used neither, so for a treat, we booked ourself into a slightly more up-market hostel and looked forward to an easy walk on the last day.

We set off from the beautiful town of Padrón, and for the first time since we crossed into Spain, the sun was peeping through the clouds even as a thin veil of mist hung over the hills across the valley. Crossing the Sar and then the N550, we first passed the church of Iria Flavia before heading away from the main road, on country lanes through Porta Dos Mariños and on towards A Escravitude, A Picaraña and eventually to Lugar de Pedreira.

Once out of Padrón, the route wandered easily through the Sar valley, home to many pretty Galician villages; the path led us through field after field of spring flowers – poppies, foxgloves and buttercups – whilst also giving us a tantalising glimpse of tomorrow's mist-covered hills in the distance. The end of the Sars valley marks the beginning of the ascent to Santiago and as expected, the path began to climb steadily until we reached the Sanctuary of A Escravitude, a shrine with a hidden fountain under its impressive stairway, which tells an interesting story about a sick man that was travelling along the Way of St. James in the hope of being healed of his dropsy, an old-fashioned term to describe the oedema often associated with heart failure. As the story goes, he stopped at the fountain to have a drink and was miraculously cured. He then said, "Thank you, Our Lady, for taking away the ailment", and out of gratitude, later returned to make a donation which allowed the shrine to be built.

We were glad that we stopped, as from here the views back were wonderful; behind us lay the valleys of Padrón and magnificent vistas of the lands of Amaía, and ahead, the route descended steeply to Angueira de Suso, before it would rise again in a steep section lasting ten miles. Our destination, however, was just outside Lugar de Pedreira about six miles on, so we dug in and trekked uphill, the last few hundred metres flattening out into a tarmacked road and winding through private residences, many of which were offering respite for pilgrims.

Despite being a relatively short stretch today, it had been mainly uphill and it felt as though the miles were catching up with us, so we were happy to stop and rest. We were also happy to see a bar and food truck attached to our accommodation, as we hadn't seen a restaurant for miles and had been wondering where we would eat. We found our bunks – superior bunks with sheets and curtains, no less – and I went for a much-needed shower. When I returned, Tony was fast asleep, snoring gently, on the bottom bunk and we had been joined by our room-mates for the night, two Irish guys who introduced themselves as Glenn and Julian, friends from Ireland who were walking their first Camino together, from Valença to Santiago.

We hit it off straight away – laughing at Tony snoring and discussing our mutual hatred of bunkbed rungs – which in turn led to a long, pleasant evening drinking wine, eating the most enormous burgers I had ever seen, and chatting late into the evening. As we chatted, we were joined, one by one, by several other people, some of whom we had become acquainted with along the way over the last couple of weeks. Glenn and Julian refreshed the bottle of wine that we had originally bought and shared with them, and further bottles were subsequently bought and shared by Sven from Sweden, Melody from Australia, a German lady whose name I can't remember (apologies) and James and Lucy, walking friends from the South of England. Needless to say, we drank far too much wine and chatted for far too long, and were all a little worse for wear by the time we retired - but we did have an early(ish) night and were confident that we would be ready for our walk into Santiago tomorrow.

Chapter 25: Delaying the end

Chapter 27

The Irish Guys

The Irish Guys, Glenn and Julian, joined us at the very end of our camino journey, but quickly became good friends.

It had been Glenn's idea to walk a camino, but similarly to Tony, he had health problems that could have caused problems, and his wife was understandably concerned about him taking the trip on his own.

Julian was not keen at first. However, his and Glenn's wives were friends, so it was almost inevitable that he was going to be roped in to accompany Glenn, and support him in achieving his dream.

They had walked from Tui. Glen (by his own admission) was not as fit as he should have been, and he saw the one hundred kilometre walk as an opportunity to kick-start a new, healthier lifestyle. He was acutely aware that he needed to prevent his health from deteriorating in order that he and his wife could enjoy seeing their grandchildren grow up.

Glenn was a biker, so did enjoy exploring the great outdoors in his beloved Northern Ireland, but knew that he needed to be more active. Julian worked hard managing his own business back in Ireland and didn't really share Glenn's camino dream, but came along to support his friend and to put Glenn's wife's mind at rest. They had both enjoyed the walk much more than they thought they would, and by the time we met them, at the albergue in Lugar de Pedreira, were already talking about doing another one next year.

Against our better judgement (they were obviously a bad influence on us), it didn't take much persuasion before we were enjoying an indulgent evening with them, taking advantage of the mobile food truck and bar as our little group of four expanded to about nine or ten pilgrims, before eventually listening to common sense and retiring at about nine o'clock.

We continued to walk with Glenn and Julian the next day, reaching the cathedral at Santiago together and celebrating with them and others that evening.

The next day we bumped into them again and swapped numbers, and I am pleased to say that we have kept in touch since. I don't doubt that we will meet up with them again one day; maybe they could introduce us to the beautiful places they described in Ireland, or we could introduce them to our lovely valley at home in Lancashire; who knows, one day we may even walk another camino together – wouldn't that be grand!

Chapter 27: The Irish Guys

Chapter 28

Life is a Pilgrimage

If there is one conclusion that I have come to over the last two weeks, it is that a pilgrimage has all of the elements of a whole life condensed into a much shorter time-frame. It has a beginning and an end, brings highs and lows and everywhere in between; it elicits hope and despair, joy and pain (both mental and physical), brings out the optimist and the pessimist in you and teaches you that you can't get through it all alone – this long, messy, unpredictable life.

So I suppose the big question is, how do we make the most of that life? How can we make it the best journey it can possibly be?

Many people talk about having a purpose in life. Leaving their mark. Making a name for themselves. Leaving a legacy. Being remembered.

It is easy to get caught up in the 'competition' that life sometimes feels like. Is your job, house, car, annual holiday destination, as impressive as other people's? Are you wearing the right clothes, getting that promotion and climbing the corporate ladder? And more recently, have you got suitably impressive photographs of your experiences to prove it on your social media page?

I have never believed that I have a defining purpose in life - I think that it is unlikely that most people will be remembered after a couple of generations have passed - moreover, I have come to believe that it is '*how*' you live your life that is more important; process, rather than purpose.

I suppose that the closest philosophy to the way I feel is Absurdism - the belief that the universe and by association, the world, is wayward, indifferent and chaotic, without any ultimate direction, purpose or meaning. If this is true, then a search for individual meaning is pointless, as we do not have any control over most of the events that will happen in our life. If we accept this, just making the best choices we can in order to improve and enhance our daily life, we can construct our own simple purpose and happiness whilst accepting that some events and other people's choices are outside of our control.

Some people function best with some sort of religious belief in their lives, to give them a structure for their meaning, either borrowed or constructed, and many people walk a Camino hoping for the inspiration to construct that meaning that they seek. Others are content to live within a moral framework, or use nature as their muse and inspiration.

Walking the Camino for just two weeks gives you time to work through questions that you may have about your life. It allows your mind to wander in a way you simply don't have time to do when faced with the busyness of work, family and social commitments. Your feet move automatically, following the yellow arrows, giving your mind the freedom to contemplate, create and even meditate; allowing the everyday sounds of birdsong, running water, footsteps, chatter (in many different languages), occasional traffic and the pitter-patter of rain, to wash over you without the need for further attention.

I have come to recognise the similarities between my Camino and the pilgrimage of my life, and it really isn't that complicated. The topography of life is like the topography of the land, ups and downs, better days and worse days. We have to learn to make the best of it all and find value in every day.

I have learned some lessons along the way, and reaffirmed some of my beliefs:

❢❣ We should expect life to be hard - it is too complicated to be anything else.

❢❣ You should learn from all of your experiences and try to be a better person through the lessons you learn.

❢❣ You should look for the good in people; listen to them and try to understand their stories.

❢❣ You should choose kindness, and help people whenever you have the power to do so.

❢❣ You should appreciate what you have. We are not all born equal in this world. If you have any advantage at all, you are privileged.

❢❣ Sometimes you can act to make things better and sometimes you just have to accept the hand you are dealt.

❢❣ It is important to listen to your body and move towards your own goals at your own pace.

- You should take pride in yourself and your own achievements.

- You should do things that make you happy and make the most of the time you have.

- You should try to take time out for yourself every day and enjoy your own headspace.

- You have to accept that you can't change the world, but you can change the way you react to its challenges.

The penultimate evening was one of our best on the Camino. A group of us: four English, one Australian, two Irish, one German and one Swedish, sat for hours over good food and many bottles of wine, talking about ourselves and our countries, politics and religion and what we liked and disliked about the world.

What became clear is that it is not ordinary people who are broken; ordinary people are inclusive, want harmony, enjoy debate and are happy to put differences aside and enjoy each other's company. All of us want a better world for our families - our children and grandchildren - we maybe just need to walk a bit further to give ourselves the headspace to figure out how to make that happen.

After all, if we cannot change what life and the world has to throw at us, then we need to be able to make the choices that enable us to grow from the experience.

"That which does not kill me makes me stronger." Nietzsche

Chapter 29

Day 13 – Santiago de Compostela

Pedreira de Lugar to Santiago de Compostela

Distance walked 12 kilometres

Just as in life, the final stage of our journey was not the prettiest, but we were determined to make the most of it and we were excited to take our final Camino steps into Santiago to collect our Compostela.

We couldn't believe it was already the last day of our hike. The two weeks had gone so quickly, and yet it felt like we'd been doing this forever, and had settled into the comforting rhythm of waking up, packing up, and starting our daily walk. So, with our collection of acquired minor injuries, but happy hearts, we set off on our final walk, a walk that was completed, rightly, with friends.

The route continued as it had ended yesterday – uphill – as we walked along tarmac roads, more rural dirt roads, through fields and under the canopy of woodlands until we reached Milladoiro, two hundred and sixty metres above sea level and the highest point of the day. It is here that pilgrims used to humiliate themselves by lying on the ground when they caught their first glimpse of the towers of the cathedral, but nowadays, the towers are not visible so thankfully we escaped the 'humiliation' ritual.

We were now only seven and a half kilometres away from our final destination, walking through the not-so-pretty satellite towns of Santiago. The downhill section took us across several complex road systems, and it did feel as though this section lasted much longer than it should have done, but we just kept going, ticking off the way-markers mile by mile.

Chatting did make the time pass more quickly though; we were walking with Glenn and Julian, the two Irish guys we had met yesterday, and we certainly kept each other going, taking turns to walk at the back to encourage a decent pace, as we wanted to arrive by twelve noon when the cathedral bells traditionally peal out to welcome pilgrims and mark the start of the pilgrim mass.

As we got closer, the route climbed once again for the final time, and the rain began to fall. This time though, we didn't mind – were almost oblivious – as the atmosphere between pilgrims on the wet pavements became charged, anticipating our arrival.

The Portuguese Way isn't the only Camino route that empties onto the cathedral square – all of the routes of Saint James end there outside the Santiago Cathedral: people who have been walking the Camino Frances, Camino Ingles, Camino Primitivo, Camino Invierno and more, and there was a great buzz of energy as we made the final approach to the cathedral square.

Even though we took a wrong turn right at the end, and approached from a different angle, I knew the moment that I saw the Cathedral of Santiago de Compostela that it would be a moment I would always remember – and right on cue, the bells began to peal out.

I'm not ashamed to admit that it was an emotional moment and, for me, felt very significant; even now, writing this chapter, I have goosebumps and can feel the emotion rising in me again. This trip had been years in the planning and we had walked for almost two hundred and fifty kilometres through two countries to get here. At one point, in the first week, we had doubted that we would even make it; but here we were, standing in the Plaza del Obradoiro amongst hundreds of other pilgrims, with the sound of the bells ringing in our ears and the extraordinary sight of the twin bell towers of the cathedral towering over us.

For a few moments we sat on the steps, not talking, just living in the moment and contemplating the enormity of our achievement, sharing it through a wave and a smile as we saw people we had met along the way. Everyone was elated and some people were emotional. Many people had removed their shoes to walk the last mile barefoot in honour of St James, and it was humbling to see how much this meant to so many people.

By this time, we had become separated from our fellow walkers, and had also missed the beginning of the pilgrim's mass, the queue being looped around the whole square.

We walked slowly around the circumference of the cathedral, taking in the magnificence of its architecture, from the thick walls and rounded arches of its original 11th century

Romanesque features, to its Baroque façade, Gothic enhancements and seventy-metre-tall twin bell towers topped with Baroque spires, all of which have been constructed, restored and preserved to varying degrees over the last thousand years. It is an exceptional blend of styles which manages to encapsulate its time's rich history and cultural significance effortlessly, whilst at the same time remaining humble and not overshadowing its spiritual importance.

Our cultural need filled, we arrived at the Pilgrim Office for the most important job of the day.

Day 13: Santiago de Compostela

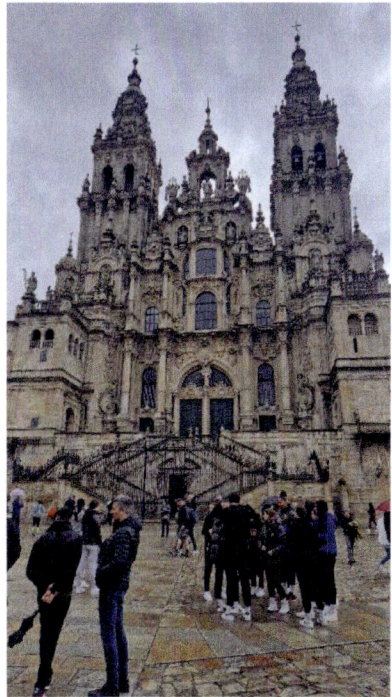

Chapter 30

The Compostela

We arrived and joined the queue at the Pilgrim Office, and when we reached the door some half an hour later, were asked our nationality and directed down a long corridor. We passed through a shady courtyard, the path looping around a fountain, and entered a stone building where our pilgrim passport was checked by a uniformed attendant. I'm not sure what I was expecting from the process – maybe a solemn 'well done' from an ancient monk who would then sign my certificate with a quill. I hadn't expected my Compostela to be processed via one of a bank of computers and then printed out on a modern printer – it would appear that the process of issuing the Compostela has been modernised since the 10th century, and is now somewhat lacking in the romance and occasion it deserves.

The process was very smooth though, and ten minutes later we were leaving with our certificates of completion - our 'Compostela'. Reunited with Glenn and Julian, and joined once again by the group we had prematurely celebrated with last night, we headed to the nearest bar for more celebratory drinks.

So why a Compostela?

Since the ninth and tenth centuries, pilgrims have been making their way to the tomb of the apostle, St James, at Santiago. At that point in time, the pilgrimage was institutionalised and took on certain social and religious considerations, and it was deemed necessary to accredit its completion.

At first, badges in the shape of a scallop shell were used that could only be acquired in Santiago. By completing your journey to Santiago de Compostela, you earned this as a literal badge of honour, and it gave you protection on your entire journey home. *Imagine having to walk all the way back now!* Sadly, the scallop shell badges were easily and eagerly falsified, with counterfeits being sold at the entrances to the city, and by the Middle Ages, it was decided that another accreditation method was needed.

From the 13th century, 'cartas probatoria' were issued. This was an official letter which provided, evidence of a completed pilgrimage issued directly from the cathedral, and in the 16th century, this became a certificate, to which certain conditions were attached and had to be proven by the pilgrim. These conditions remain to this day and are as follows:

REQUIREMENTS FOR RECEIVING THE COMPOSTELA

Once the pilgrimage is finished, along a recognised route, the Catedral de Santiago will issue the Compostela, an historical document written in Latin to award those who come to the tomb of the Apostle St James for Christian purposes.

Pilgrimage can take place on foot or horseback and consists of completion of at least 100 continuous kilometres on the same route to Santiago. The final stage must include at least, the last one leading into Santiago's Cathedral.

If a pilgrim has already started a route on foot, outside Spain but along one of the routes recognised by the International Pilgrim's Reception Office system, the required distance in Spain shall be no less than 70 kilometres.

Pilgrimage can be made by bicycle, and must be at least 200 kilometres, following the same conditions as the pilgrimage on foot.

The Cabildo (Church Council) reserves the right to grant the Compostela in special and exceptional cases, when the above distances cannot be completed. In such instances, the International Pilgrim Welcome Centre must be contacted in advance, and individual criteria agreed.

The Way can be completed in stages, provided they are in chronological and geographical order. However, if you only do the minimum required distance (last 100 or 200 kilometre), you must always get your Credencial stamped at the start and end of each stage, including the corresponding date, to show that the pilgrim has resumed the Way in the same place where they last stopped.

Children and pilgrimage. Children who make the pilgrimage with their parents or in groups, and have received the sacrament of Communion, or have the ability to understand the meaning of the spiritual or religious nature of the Way, can receive the "Compostela". If they are not mature enough due to their young age, they are given a special certificate with their names. In the case of infants or very young children, their names are included on the parent or accompanying adult's "Compostela".

The English translation of the text on the Compostela is as follows:

The Chapter of this Holy Apostolic and Metropolitan Cathedral of Compostela, custodian of the seal of the Altar of St. James, to all the Faithful and pilgrims who arrive from anywhere on the Orb of the Earth with an attitude of devotion or because of a vow or promise make a pilgrimage to the Tomb of the Apostle, Our Patron Saint and Protector of Spain, recognises before all who observe this document that: .... has devotedly visited this most sacred temple having done the last hundred kilometres on foot or on horseback or the last two hundred by bicycle with Christian sentiment (pietatis causa).

In witness whereof I present this document endorsed with the seal of this same Holy Church.

Issued in Santiago de Compostela on .... of .... year of our Lord ....

The Dean of the Cathedral of Santiago.

Chapter 30: The Compostela

Chapter 31

European Reunion

It has been a great couple of weeks and a truly wonderful experience completing this walk; not without its challenges, but worth every blister.

Several chapters back, I wrote about all the amazing people we have met along the way, yet in the last two days we have met so many more, and it has been such a privilege getting to know them.

We walked the last twelve kilometre to the cathedral in Santiago with Glenn and Julian, two great Irish guys who I've got a feeling, we are going to keep in touch with. Sometimes you just know!

Despite the after effects of all that wine, we all set off in the morning with high spirits, excited about reaching our destination. It was a first Camino for all of us and I think it's fair to say that we weren't sure how we would feel on arrival.

Despite it being uphill most of the way, and raining, there was a celebratory atmosphere as we reached the square, with pilgrims arriving from all of the Camino routes through Spain, Portugal and France; many walking much further than us, but all congratulating each other on their individual achievements.

Photographs taken and Compostela collected, we settled at a bar for a celebratory drink and were reunited, over the course of the afternoon, with many people we had met and walked with along the way, and who we ended up spending a splendid evening with, celebrating again with amazing food and more wine, late into the night.

After we had eaten, we all returned to the cathedral square, still busy and now beautifully floodlit. As the bars were all closing, we thought that we would have to say goodnight and go our own ways; all of us except Julian, that is, who disappeared into the foyer of a very posh hotel. A few moments later, he emerged, summoning us all over. He had somehow managed to persuade the manager to let us all in for a drink, and drink we did until about 3am in their very up-market lounge area – in our quite smelly, damp walking clothes. I hope the very large wine bill, and the tip we left, made it worth their while – they certainly made our day.

We said our belated goodnights and all made our way back to our accommodations. We were staying at a hostel just a few hundred yards from the cathedral square, and for once, we were the tiptoeing, giggling dirty stop-outs, trying to undress and get into our bunks as quietly as possible so that we didn't wake anyone. Not that it was likely, as the lady on the bottom bunk, below Tony, snored loudly all night before getting up and leaving for 7am mass, returning a little later to weep in her bed, unresponsive to any of our concerned enquiries. I just hope that she was overwhelmed with joy and not overtired at being woken at 3am.

So, after very little sleep, and slightly hungover, we visited the cathedral and had a last wander around the old town, picking up some souvenirs and bumping into the boys for one last drink before they left for their return flight to Ireland.

What an amazing experience! I am sure that we will keep in touch with lots of the people we have met - we have even set up a WhatsApp group - and I imagine that this will not be our last Camino. Who knows, we may all meet up one day to do another one together, wouldn't that be nice.

But first, a rest. *Buen camino*

Chapter 31: European Reunion

Chapter 32

The After-Story

Arriving at the cathedral in Santiago was an amazing feeling. The buzz, the camaraderie, the church bells...

We rested up for a couple of days in a nice little B&B a few miles outside the centre, and then it was time to go home; and as we waited at the bus station for our bus back to Porto the buzz turned to a deep lull. I wasn't the only one, there were lots of pilgrims with their backpacks and scallop shells, all of them silent. What had happened? All along the trail, just days earlier, we would have been waving, smiling at each other, chatting. We had all seen and done incredible things on the Camino; bonded over food and drink, hopes and dreams, experiences and stories; through sunshine and showers, despite broken washing machines and blisters. How could that glow fade so quickly?

To me, it felt like a loss. Tomorrow I wouldn't be here anymore. I wouldn't be doing the Camino. I wouldn't be living this life.

But over the next few weeks the glow returned. The pilgrimage doesn't end after you arrive in Santiago de Compostela, and it's not *just* a walking holiday either. It was something truly special; something I will remember and treasure for my whole life, and a feeling that I hope I will be able to recreate again – another Camino maybe.

I don't know what is next, what this unpredictable, chaotic world will throw at me in my remaining years. But I will certainly use the lessons I have learned on The Portuguese Way to help me to find my way in life; to work my way through the hard times and to make the absolute most of everything else; and if a reminder about what is important in life is needed, we can always walk another camino.

Chapter 33

Camino Reflections

We did it! 248 kilometres from cathedral to cathedral, from Porto Santiago.

I am so grateful to have been able to afford this opportunity; to have had the physical ability to complete it, to have met such amazing people on the way; and to have done it with my best friend in the whole world.

But the end of this Camino will not be the end of our pilgrimage. As I have already said, life itself is a pilgrimage, it starts when you are born and does not finish until you take your last breath. Everybody's life is a wonderful, unique journey and so everyone is a pilgrim, moving forward, step by step, through the journey of their life.

I thought a lot on my Camino, and this is what it boils down to. It's not rocket science, but it does no harm to ground yourself occasionally and remember what really matters:

- Life is a journey.
- Some parts are easy - enjoy them!
- Some parts are just OK - enjoy those parts too.
- Some parts are tough - just get through them.
- Be kind and accept kindness from others.
- Look after the people you love.
- Act responsibly and do whatever you do to the best of your ability
- Spend your money on pleasurable experiences - you can't take it with you.
- The bad things will pass and you will forget.
- The good things will pass but you will remember them.
- Enjoy today because tomorrow is not guaranteed.

And **FINALLY**, take **every** opportunity to experience happiness; enjoy that quiet moment with someone you love, that beautiful view, a cold beer, the smell of the flowers, the morning song of the birds, your favourite flavour ice-cream. Life is a journey, and as far as we know, the only one - make sure you enjoy it.

Appendix

Albergues

There are many ways to walk a camino, and whilst nobody can do the actual walking for you, there are plenty of companies out there, all of which will provide bespoke services from completely guided walks, baggage transfer deals and prebooked B&B or luxury hotel accommodation. You can also choose to complete your camino on horseback or by bicycle, and can opt to walk only the final hundred kilometres and still be assured that you will receive your Compostela on arrival in Santiago*

Having this range of options available is amazing as it makes 'doing a camino' accessible for most people, which can only be a good thing.

When planning our walk, we had already decided that we wanted to travel as authentically as possible, carrying our own packs, eating pilgrim plates, engaging with the pilgrim community and staying in traditional albergues.

I am proud to say that we managed to do all of that, and that the experience was a real pleasure.

I have listed the accommodations that we stayed in, but there are many more that I am sure will provide the same quality of accommodation and traditional experience. It is often hit-and-miss, with fate determining which Albergue you will end up in, as you are rarely able to book ahead, each offering beds on a first-come-first-served basis.

You will receive The Compostela as long as you have had your Pilgrim Passport stamped in accordance with the guidelines set out on the official website.

Name	Address	Phone	Cost (2024)
Albergue de Peregrinos do Mosteiro de Vairão	Rua do Convento, 21 4485 Vairão	+351 256 837 240	€10 pp (donation)
O Palhuço Pilgrims Hostel	R. de Santa Leocádia 662, 4755-392 Pedra Furada	+351 252 954 331	€10 pp
Albergue Casa da Recoleta	Rua da Recoleta, 100 4750-714 Portela de Tamel	+351 253 137 075	€5 pp
The Pilgrim's hostel in Ponte de Lima	Largo Dr. Alexandre Herculano 4990-154 Ponte de Lima	+351 925 40 31 64	€5 pp
Albergue de Peregrinos in Rubiães	Estrada S. Pedro Rubiães, 949, 4940-686, Portugal	+351 965 053 751	€10 pp
Albergue de Peregrinos in Tui	R. Párroco Rodríguez Vázquez, 0, 36700 Tui, Pontevedra, Spain	+34 649 502 704	€10 pp
Albergue Buen Camino in Tui	Avenida de la Concordia, 10, Tui, 36700, Spain	+34 986 60 40 52	€25 pp
Albergue Santa Ana De Veigadaña en Mos	Camiño de Sta. Ana, 11, 36416, Pontevedra, Spain	+34 673 28 94 91	€8 pp
Bulezen Urban Hostel, Pontevedre	Rúa García Camba 12 - PISO 1º, 36001, Pontevedra	+34 886 06 02 07	€30 pp
Albergue GBC Caldas	Calle Las Silgadas Nr.16 Caldas de Reis, 36650	+34 604 05 37 29	€22 pp
Albergue de peregrinos de Padrón	Rúa Costiña do Carme, 0, 15900 Padrón, A Coruña	+34 673 65 61 73	€10 pp
Albergue Aldea da Pedreira	Aldea Pedreira, 90, 15866 Teo, A Coruña, Spain	+34 619 54 49 66	€10 pp

ABOUT THE AUTHOR

Diane Neilson is a mum of three and retired teacher who, at last, has time to focus on her own passions: walking, reading and writing.

After living in a large town for most of her life, she now lives with her husband in Lancashire in a picture-postcard stone cottage with a beautiful garden, enjoying and writing about her daily walks in the North of England, and further afield when on holiday.

Her inspirations come from her observations and thoughts when walking and from everyday interactions with ordinary people, and often lead to ideas for her poetry and short stories.

Walking the Portuguese Way, in May 2024 was a perfect opportunity to combine two of her passions, walking and writing, and prompted her to write her first travel memoir, 'Everybody should walk a Camino.'

Printed in Dunstable, United Kingdom